Strategic Business Reporting (SBR)

Pocket Notes

KAPLAN PUBLISHING

British library cataloguing-in-publication data

A catalogue record for this book is available from the British Library.

Published by:
Kaplan Publishing UK
Unit 2 The Business Centre
Molly Millars Lane
Wokingham
Berkshire
RG41 2QZ

ISBN 978-1-83735-037-7

© Kaplan Financial Limited, 2025

Printed and bound in Great Britain.

The text in this material and any others made available by any Kaplan Group company does not amount to advice on a particular matter and should not be taken as such. No reliance should be placed on the content as the basis for any investment or other decision or in connection with any advice given to third parties. Please consult your appropriate professional adviser as necessary. Kaplan Publishing Limited, all other Kaplan group companies, the International Accounting Standards Board, and the IFRS Foundation expressly disclaim all liability to any person in respect of any losses or other claims, whether direct, indirect, incidental, consequential or otherwise arising in relation to the use of such materials. Printed and bound in Great Britain.

Acknowledgements

This product contains copyright material and trademarks of the IFRS Foundation®. All rights reserved. Used under licence from the IFRS Foundation®. Reproduction and use rights are strictly limited. For more information about the IFRS Foundation and rights to use its material please visit www.ifrs.org.

Disclaimer: To the extent permitted by applicable law the Board and the IFRS Foundation expressly disclaims all liability howsoever arising from this publication or any translation thereof whether in contract, tort or otherwise (including, but not limited to, liability for any negligent act or omission) to any person in respect of any claims or losses of any nature including direct, indirect, incidental or consequential loss, punitive damages, penalties or costs.

Information contained in this publication does not constitute advice and should not be substituted for the services of an appropriately qualified professional. No part of this publication may be reproduced, stored in a retrieval system, or transmitted in any form or by any means, electronic, mechanical, photocopying, recording, or otherwise, without prior written permission of Kaplan Publishing and the IFRS Foundation.

The IFRS Foundation logo, the IASB logo, the ISSB logo, the IFRS for SMEs logo, the 'Hexagon Device', 'IFRS Foundation', 'IAS', 'IASB', 'IFRS for SMEs', 'IASs', 'IFRS', 'IFRSs', 'International Accounting Standards' and 'International Financial Reporting Standards', 'IFRIC', NIIF® and 'SIC' are **Trade Marks** of the IFRS Foundation.

The Foundation has trade marks registered around the world (**'Trade Marks'**) including 'IAS®', 'IASB®', 'IFRIC®', 'IFRS®', the IFRS® logo, 'IFRS for SMEs®', ISSB ®, IFRS for SMEs® logo, the 'Hexagon Device', 'International Financial Reporting Standards®', NIIF® and 'SIC®'.

Further details of the Foundation's Trade Marks are available from the Licensor on request.

This Product includes content from the International Ethics Standards Board for Accountants (IESBA), published by the International Federation of Accountants (IFAC) in 2017 and is used with permission of IFAC.

This Product includes content from the International Auditing and Assurance Standards Board (IAASB), published by the International Federation of Accountants (IFAC) in 2017 and is used with permission of IFAC.

© Financial Reporting Council Ltd.
This publication contains copyright material of the Financial Reporting Council Ltd. All rights reserved. No permission granted to third parties to reproduce or distribute without permission of the Financial Reporting Council Ltd.

Contents

This document references IFRS® Accounting Standards, which are authored by the International Accounting Standards Board (the Board), and published in the 2024 IFRS Accounting Standards Red Book.

The exam

Paper background

The exam requires students to examine corporate reporting from a number of perspectives. Students will be required to assess and evaluate reporting decisions made by management, their implications for a range of stakeholders, and the professional and ethical issues raised. Students are expected to be able to prepare and discuss consolidated financial statements. Knowledge of changes and developments in financial reporting is also required.

Exam format

The exam is three hours and fifteen minutes. All questions are compulsory.

Section A (50%) consists of two scenario based questions. The first question will be based on group financial statements and will include a pre-populated spreadsheet that contains a draft consolidated financial statement. One of the requirements will be to adjust this draft statement for a range of issues. The first question is also likely to test some financial reporting issues. The second question will require consideration of the reporting and ethical implications of specific events.

Section B (50%) consists of two questions. These will be scenario-based and could deal with any part of the syllabus. Section B will always include a full question or part of a question that tests the interpretation section of the syllabus.

Keys to success in SBR

- Read widely
- Study the whole syllabus
- Do not neglect the 'softer' topics – analysis and changes and developments in financial reporting are core parts of the syllabus
- Manage your time carefully to ensure that you finish the paper
- Knowledge of the accounting standards is not enough. You must be able to apply the standards to unfamiliar scenarios
- Practice exam questions to time.

Quality and accuracy are of the utmost importance to us so if you spot an error in any of our products, please send an email to mykaplanreporting@kaplan.com with full details, or follow the link to the feedback form in MyKaplan.

Our Quality Co-ordinator will work with our technical team to verify the error and take action to ensure it is corrected in future editions.

chapter

1

Frameworks

In this chapter

- *Conceptual Framework.*
- Materiality.
- IFRS 13 *Fair Value Measurement.*

The Conceptual Framework

Exam focus

The *Conceptual Framework* is an important topic in SBR and is tested on a regular basis.

Purposes

The key purposes of the Conceptual Framework are to assist:

- the Board when developing new IFRS Accounting Standards
- preparers of financial statements when no IFRS Accounting Standard applies to a transaction, or when an IFRS Accounting Standard offers a choice of accounting policy
- all parties when understanding and interpreting IFRS Accounting Standards.

The purpose of financial reporting

The purpose of financial reporting is to provide information to current and potential investors, lenders and other creditors that will enable them to make decisions about providing economic resources to an entity.

User groups need information to assess:

- an entity's potential future cash flows, and
- management's stewardship of the entity's economic resources.

This information is provided in financial statements.

Qualitative characteristics

Key Point

Financial information is only useful if it embodies the fundamental characteristics.

The enhancing characteristics make financial information more useful.

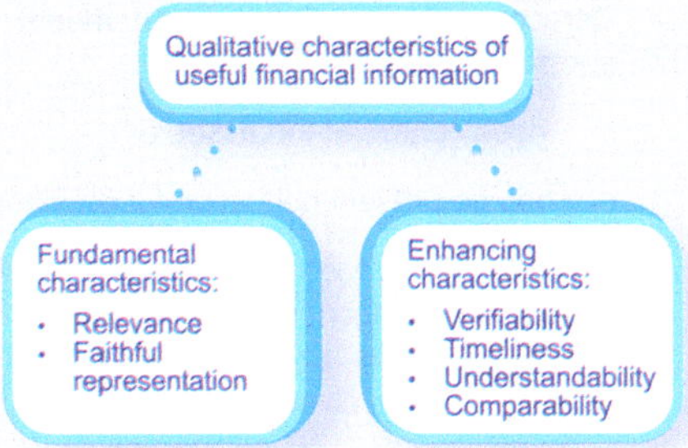

The elements

Definition

The elements are the building blocks of financial statements.

An economic resource is a **'right that has the potential to produce economic benefits'**
(para 4.4).

Asset	**'A present economic resource controlled by an entity as a result of a past event'** (para 4.3).
Liability	**'A present obligation of the entity to transfer an economic resource as a result of a past event'** (para 4.26).
Equity	The residual interest in the net assets of an entity.
Income	Increases in assets or decreases in liabilities that result in an increase to equity (excluding contributions from equity holders).
Expenses	Decreases in assets or increases in liabilities that result in decreases to equity (excluding distributions to equity holders).

Recognition

Items are recognised in financial statements if:

- they meet the definition of an element, and
- recognition provides relevant information, and
- recognition faithfully represents the entity's financial performance and position.

Derecognition

Derecognition from financial statements normally occurs when the entity:

- loses control of the asset, or
- has no present obligation for the liability.

Accounting for derecognition should faithfully represent the changes in an entity's net assets, as well as any assets or liabilities retained. This involves:

- derecognising any transferred, expired or consumed component, and
- recognising a gain or loss on the above, and
- recognising any retained component.

Measurement

If recognised in the financial statements, an element must be quantified.

The *Conceptual Framework* outlines two measurement bases:

- historical cost
- current value (this includes fair value, value-in-use, and current cost).

When selecting a measurement basis, relevance is maximised if the following are considered:

- the characteristics of the asset or liability
- how the asset or liability contributes to future cash flows.

Presentation and disclosure

The statement of profit or loss is the primary source of information about an entity's financial performance. Income and expenses should normally be recognised in this statement.

The Board might require an income or expense to be presented in other comprehensive income if it results from remeasuring an item to current value and if this means that:

- profit or loss provides more relevant information, or
- a more faithful representation is provided of an entity's performance.

Income and expenditure included in other comprehensive income should be reclassified to profit or loss when doing so results in profit or loss providing more relevant information.

Materiality

Materiality is an important concept in financial reporting, but users and preparers of financial statements require more guidance on how to apply it. The Board has published guidance in a Practice Statement.

Definition

An item is material if omitting, misstating or obscuring it would influence the economic decisions of financial statement users.

Materiality judgements are required throughout the process of preparing financial statements:

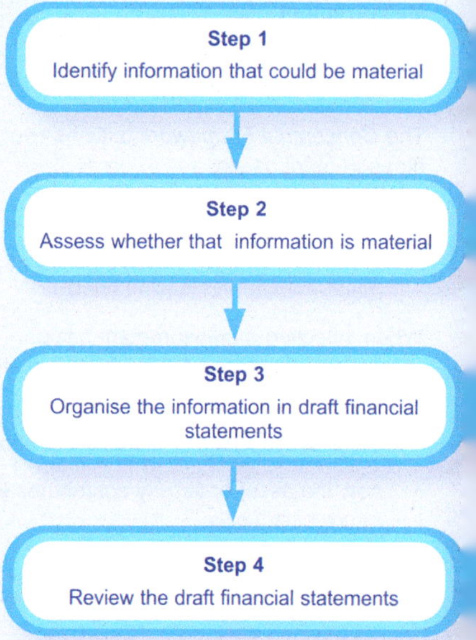

When assessing whether information is material, an entity should consider:

- Quantitative factors – measures of revenue, profit, assets, and cash flows.
- Qualitative factors – related party transactions, unusual transactions, geography, and wider economic uncertainty.

An entity only needs to apply the recognition, measurement and disclosure criteria in an IFRS Accounting Standard when the effects are material.

IFRS 13 Fair Value Measurement

Definition

Fair value is defined as '**the price that would be received to sell an asset or paid to transfer a liability in an orderly transaction between market participants at the measurement date**' (IFRS 13, para 9).

Fair value hierarchy

Level 1 inputs

- Quoted prices for identical assets in active markets

Level 2 inputs

- Quoted prices for identical assets in less active markets
- Quoted prices for similar assets in active markets

Level 3 inputs

- Unobservable inputs

Priority is given to level 1 inputs when determining fair value.

Markets

Key Point

IFRS 13 says that fair value should be determined by reference to the principal market.

This is the market with the greatest volume of activity.

If the principal market cannot be determined then fair value should be measured based on the price in the most advantageous market.

Non-financial assets

Non-financial assets include:

- Property, plant and equipment
- Intangible assets

The fair value of a non-financial asset should be based on its **highest and best use.**

Exam focus

Exam Kit questions in this area

- Juan
- Wing
- Cial
- Maple

chapter

2

The professional and ethical duty of the accountant

In this chapter

- Overview.
- Ethical issues facing the accountant.
- Ethical codes of conduct.
- Consequences of unethical behaviour.

Overview

Exam focus

Question 2 in the SBR exam will test the reporting and ethical implications of specific events in a contemporary scenario. Two professional marks will be awarded in this question.

Ethical issues facing the accountant

Definition

Professional ethics are the principles and standards that underlie the responsibilities and conduct of a person in performing his/her function in a particular field of expertise.

- Ethical principles are important in a business organisation as they set the tone for the culture and behaviour of employees and management.
- The application of ethics can sometimes be intangible. Ethics is often described as 'doing the right thing' but this can mean different things to different individuals.

- The use of digital technologies by accountants increases the range of ethical issues they may face. This includes the need for accountants to become proficient with new software and understand relevant laws and regulations around data security.

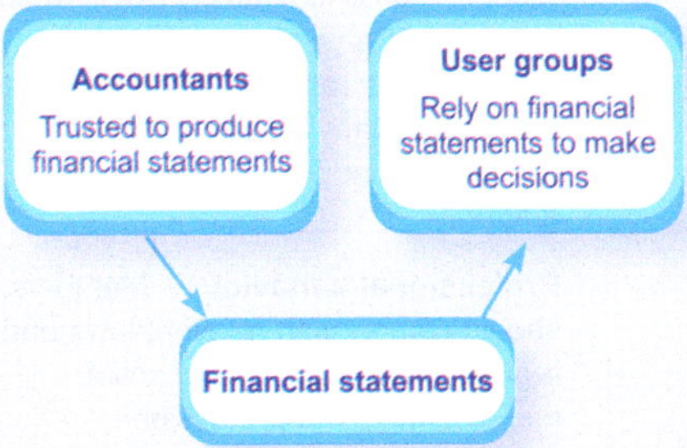

Ethical codes of conduct

Professional accountants are bound by their Institute or Association's code of ethics and are expected to act in accordance with such codes of conduct.

ACCA Code of Ethics

The ACCA Code of Ethics and Conduct applies to all students, associates and members. The Code is in the form of a framework and adopts a principles-based approach; whilst some specific rules are included, compliance is largely concerned with the observation of the fundamental principles.

- **Integrity** – Members should be straightforward and honest in all professional and business relationships.
- **Objectivity** – Members should not allow bias, conflicts of interest or undue influence of others to override their judgement.
- **Professional competence and due care** – Members have a continuing duty to maintain professional knowledge and skill at a level required to ensure that a client or employer receives a competent and professional service.
- **Confidentiality** – Members should respect the confidentiality of information acquired as a result of professional and business relationships and should not disclose any such information to third parties without proper and specific authority.
- **Professional behaviour** – Members should comply with relevant laws and regulations and avoid any action that discredits the profession.

Consequences of unethical behaviour

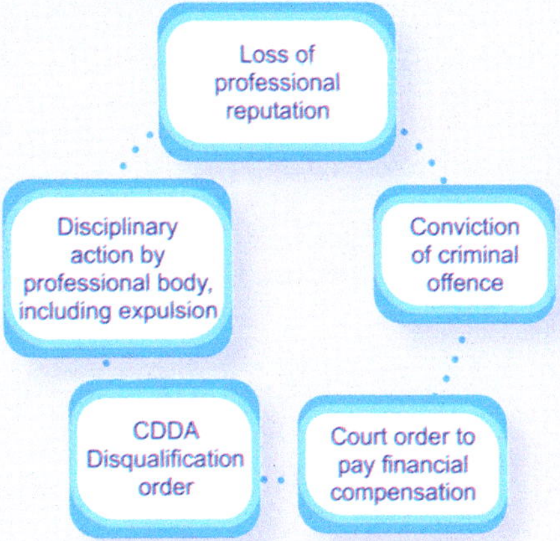

Exam focus

Exam Kit questions in this area:

- Jassie
- Renshu
- Cutherd
- Dario
- Abasi
- Apaniiwa

chapter

3

Performance reporting

In this chapter

- Overview.
- IFRS 18 *Presentation and Disclosure in Financial Statements.*
- Statement of profit or loss.
- Statement of financial position.
- Disclosure notes.
- IAS 8 *Basis of Preparation of Financial Statements.*
- IFRS 5 *Non-current Assets Held for Sale and Discontinued Operations.*
- IAS 34 *Interim Financial Reporting.*

Overview

Exam focus

- Many of these accounting standards were covered in your previous studies.
- IFRS 18 replaces IAS 1 *Presentation of Financial Statements*, which you will have seen in your prior studies.
- The level of application required in this exam will be much higher.

IFRS 18 *Presentation and Disclosure in Financial Statements*

Per IFRS 18, the objective of financial statements is to provide useful information to the users of the financial statements to help them assess:

- an entity's potential future cash flows, and
- management's stewardship of the entity's economic resources.

Role of the primary financial statements and notes

In order to provide useful information to users, entities should:

- present material information in the primary financial statements, or
- disclose material information in the notes.

To determine whether to provide information in the primary financial statements or whether to disclose in the notes, an entity should understand that each area performs a different role. These roles are as follows:

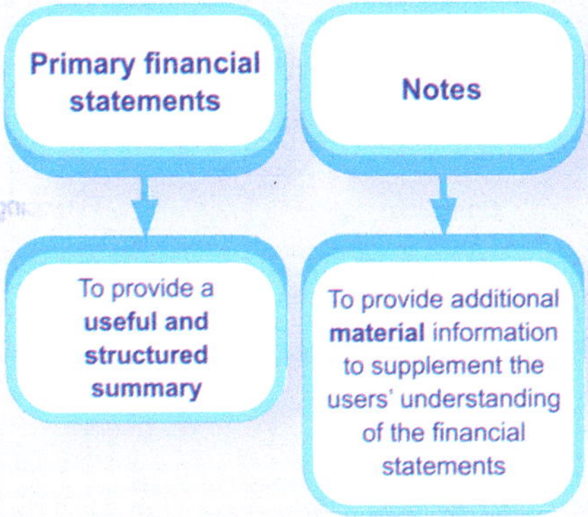

General features of financial statements

IFRS 18 requires that certain principles be followed in the preparation of the financial statements.

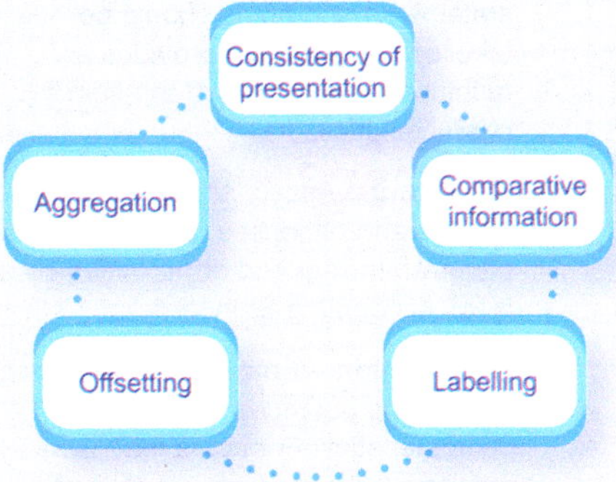

- **Consistency of presentation** – The presentation, disclosure and classification of items in the financial statements should be retained from one period to the next, unless it is clear that a change will result in a more appropriate presentation, or a change is required by an IFRS Accounting Standard.

- **Comparative information** – Comparative information for the previous period should be disclosed.
- **Labelling** – Items in the financial statements and notes should be labelled in a way that provides a faithful representation of the item's characteristics.
- **Offsetting** – Assets and liabilities, and income and expenses, should only be offset when required or permitted by an IFRS Accounting Standard.
- **Aggregation** – Entities should aggregate items if the balances have shared characteristics. For items that have characteristics that are not shared, the balances should be disaggregated.

Statement of profit or loss

IFRS 18 requires income and expenses in the statement of profit or loss to be classified into one of five categories:

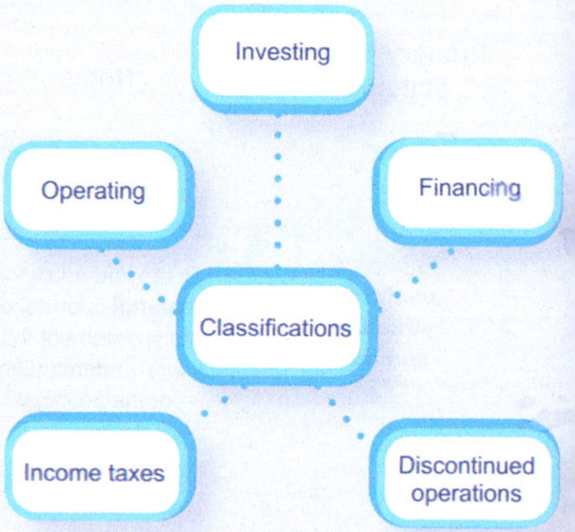

Key Point

In the SBR exam, when explaining the financial reporting treatment of a transaction, you will need to identify which categories the relevant income and expenses should be classified in.

Assuming the main business activities of an entity are not performing investing or financing activities, the typical IFRS 18 classification of income and expenses under the 3 main headings are as follows:

Category	Income and expenses from:	Examples
Operating	• Anything not classified as investing or financing • Main business activities	• Revenue • Cost of sales • Depreciation • Gains/losses on disposal of PPE • Current and past service cost from a defined benefit plan.
Investing	• Associates and joint ventures • Cash and cash equivalents • Other assets that generate a return individually and independently from other resources e.g. financial assets	• Share of associate's profit • Interest income • Transaction costs and fair value movements on FVPL financial assets.
Financing	• Liabilities that involve only the raising of finance • Liabilities that do not involve only the raising of finance	• Interest expense on financial liabilities measured at amortised cost • Unwinding of discount on provisions • Interest on lease liabilities.

Mandatory subtotals

IFRS 18 requires entities to present three mandatory subtotals in the statement of profit or loss:

- Operating profit or loss
- Profit or loss before financing and income taxes
- Profit for the year.

Presentation of operating expenses

IFRS 18 allows entities to present operating expenses based on:

- the function of the expenses within the entity, or
- the nature of the expenses, or
- a combination of the two.

An entity will choose the presentation that it feels will provide the most useful structured summary.

Advantages of presenting operating expenses:

By function	By nature
Improves comparability of expenses between different entities	Provides detailed breakdown of operating expenses
Enables performance analysis of specific business activities and functions	Enhanced transparency of costs incurred by entity
Provides greater insight into resource allocation across different functions	May help users forecast expenses in future

Statement of profit or loss for entities with specified main business activities

Entities involved in investing in particular types of assets or providing financing as a main business activity will classify some of their income and expenses differently in order to reflect their operating activities.

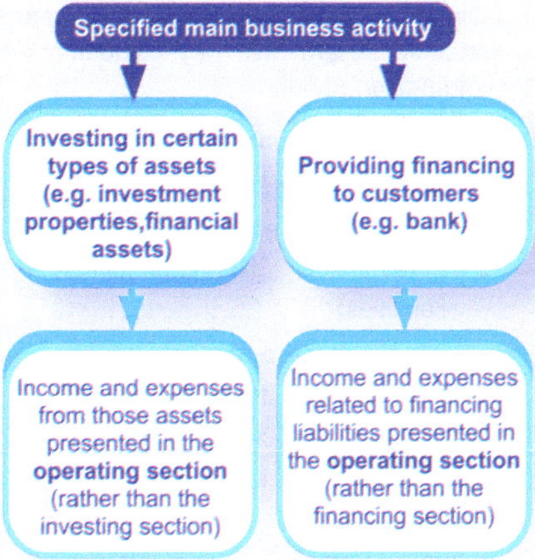

Profit or loss and other comprehensive income (OCI)

According to the *Conceptual Framework*, profit or loss is the primary source of information about an entity's financial performance during the period.

OCI are income and expenses that, in accordance with IFRS Accounting Standards, are recognised outside of profit or loss.

Items of OCI must be presented as either:

- items that might be reclassified to profit or loss in the future
- items that will not be reclassified to profit or loss in the future

Statement of financial position

Assets and liabilities must be classified as current or non-current.

Definition

A current asset is an asset that:

- will be realised or consumed during the entity's normal trading cycle, or
- it is held for trading, or
- will be realised within 12 months of the reporting date.

A current liability is a liability that:

- will be settled during the entity's normal trading cycle, or
- it is held for trading, or
- will be settled within 12 months of the reporting date
- the entity does not have the right as at the reporting date to defer settlement beyond 12 months.

Goodwill

Goodwill should be presented as a separate line item on the face of the statement of financial position, rather than being combined with other intangible assets.

Disclosure notes

Disclosure notes supplement the primary financial statements. They include important information about:

- material accounting policies
- sources of uncertainty
- valuation and estimation techniques
- unrecognised items (such as contingent liabilities)
- events after the reporting period.

Disclosure notes should be ordered systematically. This might mean:

- displaying the most relevant issues prominently

- grouping similar items together
- following the order in which items are presented in the primary financial statements.

Management-defined performance measures

IFRS 18 requires specific disclosures in respect of management-defined performance measures.

A management-defined performance measure (MPM) is a subtotal of income and expenses that:

- is used in public communications
- is used to communicate the management's view of performance to users
- is not an existing or commonly used subtotal in the statement of profit or loss.

For each measure, using a single disclosure note, an entity will need to disclose:

- a description of what part of the entity's performance is reflected by the measure and why management believe that the MPM provides useful information about the entity's performance
- how the MPM has been calculated
- a reconciliation between the MPM and the most closely related subtotal or total that is covered by an IFRS Accounting Standard
- the impact on income tax and non-controlling interests for each item disclosed in the reconciliation, and
- a description of how the income tax impact has been determined.

The disclosure note should also state that the MPMs provide management's view of an element of the entity's performance and that MPMs may not be directly comparable to other entities who disclose similar performance measures.

IAS 8 *Basis of Preparation of Financial Statements*

General presentation concepts

IAS 8 covers some general presentation concepts that have been transferred across from the now obsolete IAS 1.

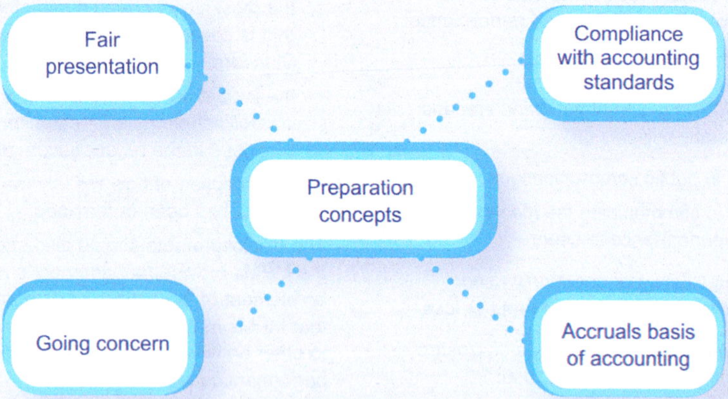

Selecting accounting policies

Accounting policies must be determined by applying the relevant IFRS Accounting Standard. If there is no standard, then management should choose an accounting policy that results in relevant and reliable financial information.

Changing accounting policies

Accounting policies can only change if:

- the change is required by a standard or interpretation; or
- the change results in more relevant and reliable information.

Changes in accounting policies are accounted for retrospectively as if the new policy had always been applied.

Accounting Estimates

Accounting estimates are amounts that are subject to measurement uncertainty, such as:

- the measurement of a warranty provision
- depreciation of property, plant and equipment during the reporting period.

Changes in accounting estimates are accounted for prospectively.

Errors

Prior period errors are misstatements due to mistakes in applying accounting policies and fraud. They are corrected retrospectively.

IFRS 5 Non-current Assets Held for Sale and Discontinued Operations

Definition

Per IFRS 5, a discontinued operation is a component of an entity that has been sold, or which is classified as held for sale, and which is

- a separate line of business, or
- part of a plan to dispose of a separate line of business, or
- a subsidiary acquired solely for resale.

Presentation

A **single amount** for discontinued operations is presented on the face of the statement of profit or loss. This comprises:

- the post-tax profit or loss of the operation
- any profit or loss on disposal, or any loss on classification as held for sale.

Example statement of profit or loss showing discontinued operation

	20X2	20X1
	$m	$m
Revenue	200	190
Operating expenses	(40)	(50)
Operating profit	160	140
Interest expense	(20)	(20)
Profit before financing and income taxes	140	120
Income tax expense	(30)	(25)
Profit from continuing operations	110	95
Discontinued operations		
Loss from discontinued operations	(70)	(50)
Profit for the period	40	45

IAS 34 *Interim Financial Reporting*

Definition

An interim period '**is a financial reporting period that is shorter than a full financial year**' (IAS 34, para 4).

IAS 34 outlines the minimum content that should be included in an interim financial report.

The minimum content to be included is:

- A condensed statement of financial position.
- A condensed statement of profit or loss and other comprehensive income.
- A condensed statement of changes in equity.
- A condensed statement of cash flows.
- Selected disclosure notes.

Exam Focus

Exam Kit questions in this area:

- Sterling
- Renshu
- Wing
- Abasi
- Maple
- Jobon
- Cial

chapter

4

Revenue

In this chapter

- Revenue recognition.
- Identify the contract.
- Identify the performance obligations.
- Determine the transaction price.
- Allocate the transaction price.
- Recognise revenue.
- Contract costs.

Revenue recognition

IFRS 15 *Revenue from Contracts with Customers* adopts a five step approach to revenue recognition:

(1) Identify the contract with a customer

↓

(2) Identify the performance obligations within the contract

↓

(3) Determine the transaction price

↓

(4) Allocate the transaction price to the performance obligations within the contract

↓

(5) Recognise revenue when or as a performance obligation is satisfied

Identify the contract

IFRS 15 *Revenue from Contracts with Customers* says that a contract is an agreement between two parties that creates rights and obligations.

An entity can only account for revenue from a contract if it meets the following criteria:

- the parties have approved the contract and each party's rights can be identified
- payment terms can be identified
- the contract has commercial substance
- it is probable that the selling entity will receive consideration.

Identify the performance obligations

The distinct performance obligations within a contract must be identified.

Definition

Performance obligations are promises to transfer distinct goods or services to a customer.

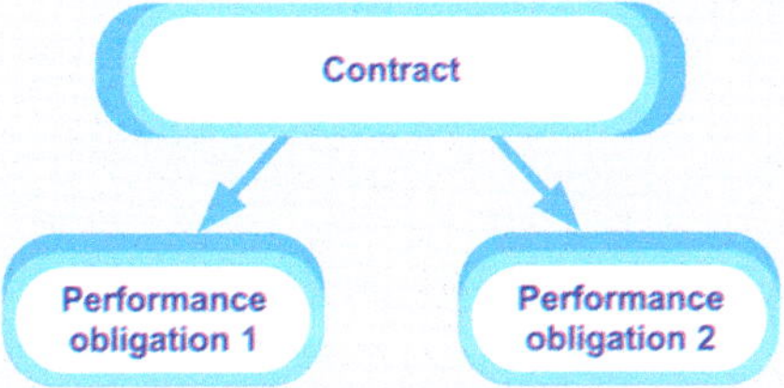

Entities must determine the nature of their performance obligation. They might be:

- a **principal** (providing the good or service)
- an **agent** (arranging for the good or service to be provided by another party).

An entity is the principal if it controls the good or service before it is transferred to the buyer.

Determine the transaction price

Definition

The transaction price is the consideration that the selling entity will be entitled to once it has fulfilled the performance obligations in the contract.

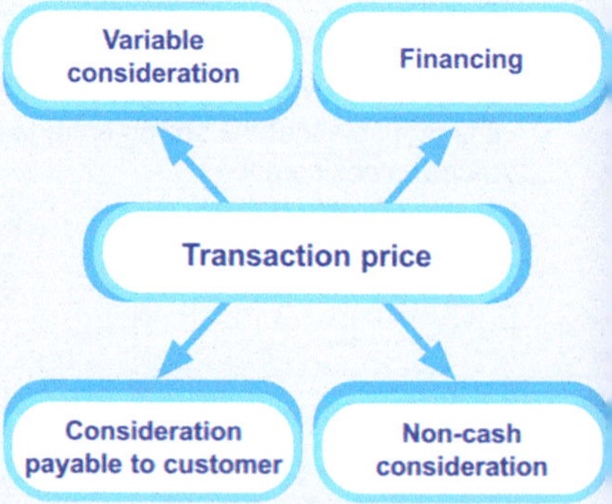

Variable consideration (i.e. a bonus or a penalty)

The seller must estimate the amount expected to be received.

This estimate is included in the transaction price if it is **highly probable** that a **significant reversal in the amount of revenue recognised will not occur** when the uncertainty is resolved.

Financing

If there is a significant financing component, the consideration receivable must be discounted to present value.

Non-cash consideration

This is measured at fair value.

Consideration payable to a customer

This is deducted from the transaction price.

Allocate the transaction price

Key Point

The total transaction price should be allocated to each performance obligation in proportion to standalone selling prices.

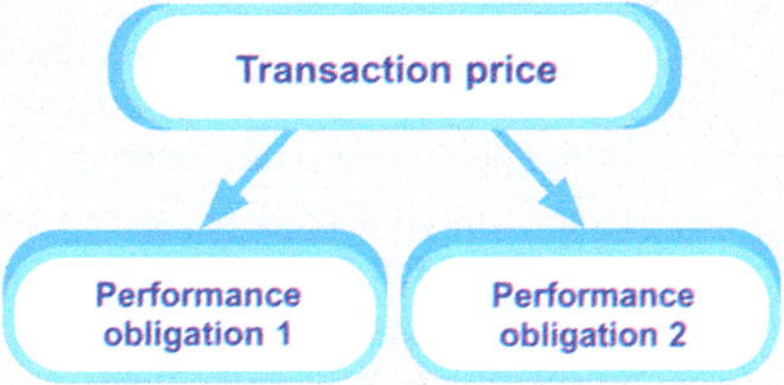

Recognise revenue

Key Point

Revenue is recognised when (or as) the entity satisfies a performance obligation.

An entity only satisfies a performance obligation over time if one of the following criteria is met:

- the customer simultaneously receives and consumes the benefits from the entity's performance as it performs
- the entity is creating or enhancing an asset controlled by the customer
- the entity cannot use the asset 'for an alternative use' and the entity can demand payment for its performance to date.

If a performance obligation is **satisfied over time**, then revenue is recognised based on the progress towards completion.

If a performance obligation is not satisfied over time then it is satisfied at **a point in time**. This is normally when the customer **obtains control** of the promised asset.

Contract costs

An entity must capitalise:

- the costs of obtaining a contract
- the costs of fulfilling a contract that do not fall within the scope of another standard (such as IAS 2 Inventories).

Exam focus

Exam Kit questions in this area include:

- Jassie
- Rubul
- Luna
- Bohai
- Jacinta
- Abasi
- Cial

chapter

5

Non-current assets

In this chapter

- Overview.
- IAS 16 *Property, Plant and Equipment.*
- IAS 20 *Accounting for Government Grants and Disclosure of Government Assistance.*
- IAS 23 *Borrowing Costs.*
- IAS 40 *Investment Property.*
- IAS 38 *Intangible Assets.*
- IAS 36 *Impairment of Assets.*
- IFRS 5 *Non-current Assets Held for Sale.*

Overview

Exam focus

- This chapter focuses on standards relating to tangible and intangible assets.
- All of these have been studied previously but are regularly examined.
- This chapter is a reminder of the key points.

IAS 16 *Property, Plant and Equipment*

Key Point

Property, plant and equipment is initially recognised at cost.

Subsequent expenditure on non-current assets may be capitalised if it:

- enhances the economic benefits of the asset, e.g. adding a new wing to a building
- replaces part of an asset that has been separately depreciated, and has been fully depreciated e.g. a furnace that requires new linings
- replaces economic benefits previously consumed, e.g. a major inspection of aircraft.

The asset is depreciated over its useful life.

- The **depreciation method** and **useful life** of an asset should be reviewed at the end of each year.
- If an asset has parts with **different lives**, (e.g. a building with a flat roof), the component parts of the asset should be depreciated separately.

Revaluation of property, plant and equipment

Revaluation to fair value is **optional**. If one asset is revalued, all assets in that class must be revalued.

- Revaluation **gains** are credited to other comprehensive income unless the gain reverses a previous revaluation loss of the same asset previously recognised in profit or loss.
- Revaluation **losses** are charged to the statement of profit or loss (operating section) unless the loss relates to a previous revaluation surplus, in which case it should be charged to other comprehensive income.
- The revised carrying amount is depreciated over the remaining useful life of the asset.
- An entity may choose to make a **reserves transfer** for the **excess depreciation** arising from a revaluation. This is taken from the revaluation surplus to retained earnings.

IAS 20 Accounting for Government Grants and Disclosure of Government Assistance

Key Point

Grants should not be recognised until there is reasonable assurance that the grant will be received and that conditions will be complied with.

- Income grants given to subsidise expenditure should be matched to the related costs.
- Grants for purchases of non-current assets should be recognised over the expected useful lives of the related assets. There are two acceptable accounting policies for this:
  - deduct the grant from the cost of the asset and depreciate the net cost; or
  - treat the grant as deferred income and release to the statement of profit or loss (operating section) over the life of the asset.

IAS 23 *Borrowing Costs*

Definition

Borrowing costs are interest and other costs incurred when borrowing funds.

Entities **must capitalise** borrowing costs that are directly attributable to the acquisition, construction or production of assets that take a substantial amount of time to get ready for use.

IAS 40 *Investment Property*

Definition

Investment property is property held to earn rentals or for capital appreciation or both.

Investment property is initially recognised at cost.

An entity can then choose either the **cost model** (cost less depreciation) or the **fair value model**.

- The **fair value model** recognises investment properties in the statement of financial position at **fair value. Gains** and **losses** on remeasurement are recognised in the **statement of profit or loss**, typically in the investing section.

IAS 38 *Intangible Assets*

Definition

An **intangible asset 'is an identifiable non-monetary asset without physical substance**' (IAS 38, para 8).

- An intangible asset is initially recognised at cost if:

  (1) It is identifiable.

  (2) It is controlled by the entity.

  (3) It will generate probable future economic benefits for the entity.

  (4) The cost can be measured reliably.

- If an intangible does not meet the recognition criteria, then it should be charged to the statement of profit or loss (operating section) as expenditure is incurred.
- Intangible assets should be amortised over their useful lives.
- If it can be demonstrated that the useful life is indefinite then no amortisation should be charged but an annual impairment review must be carried out.
- Intangible assets can be revalued but only if fair values can be determined with reference to an active market.
- Costs incurred during the research must be expensed as they are incurred. Costs incurred during development should be recognised as an asset if they meet the following criteria:

  (a) the project is technically feasible

  (b) the asset will be completed then used or sold

  (c) the entity is able to use or sell the asset

(d) the asset will generate future economic benefits

(e) the entity has adequate technical, financial and other resources to complete the project

(f) the expenditure on the project can be reliably measured.

- Amortisation over the useful life of the new product or process will commence once the project is complete.

IAS 36 *Impairment of Assets*

Definition

An **impairment loss** is the amount by which the carrying amount of an asset or cash-generating unit exceeds its recoverable amount.

Impairment is measured by comparing the carrying amount of an asset with its recoverable amount.

Key Point

If the carrying amount exceeds the recoverable amount, the asset is impaired and must be written down.

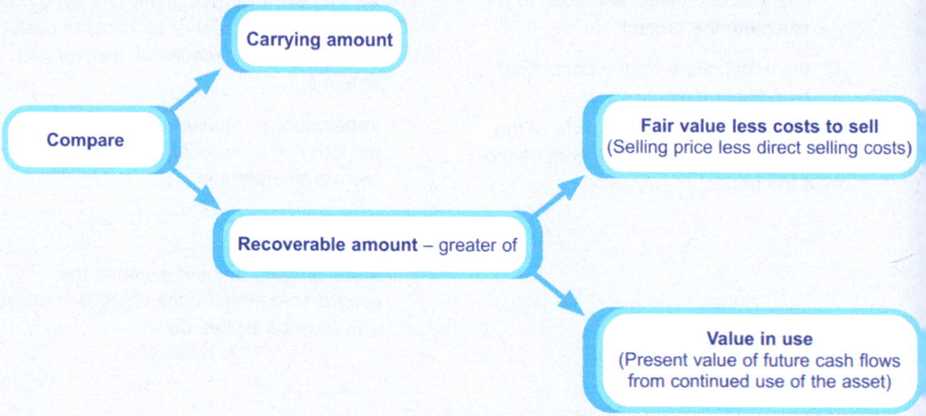
Carrying amount
Compare
Recoverable amount – greater of
Fair value less costs to sell
(Selling price less direct selling costs)
Value in use
(Present value of future cash flows from continued use of the asset)

Indicators of impairment

Impairment reviews are required where there is an indicator of impairment.

Internal Indicators:

- Physical damage to the asset.
- Management committed to reorganisation of the business.
- Idle or obsolete assets.
- Operating losses in the business where the assets are used.

External Indicators:

- Competitor actions.
- Increasing interest rates (because this reduces the value in use).
- Market values of assets falling.

Cash-generating units (CGU)

Key Point

Individual assets may not generate a distinguishable cash flow. In this case the impairment calculation should be based on a CGU.

Definition

A **cash-generating unit** is the smallest group of assets that generates independent cash inflows.

Impairment losses on a CGU are allocated in the following order:

(1) goodwill

(2) remaining assets in proportion to carrying amounts.

No asset can be written down below the higher of fair value less costs to sell, value in use and zero.

Recognition of impairment losses

Assets held at cost: The amount of the impairment is charged to the statement of profit or loss (operating section).

Revalued assets: The impairment is charged to other comprehensive income to reverse any previous surplus on that asset with any excess charged to profit or loss.

IFRS 5 *Non-current Assets Held for Sale*

Definition

An asset should be classified as held for sale if its carrying amount will be recovered principally through a sales transaction.

To be classified as held for sale, the following criteria must be met:

- The asset must be available for sale in its present condition.
- The sale must be highly probable.
- Management must be committed to the sale.
- The asset should be actively marketed at a reasonable price.
- The sale must be expected within a year.

If the criteria are met:

- The asset should be measured at the lower of carrying amount and fair value less costs to sell.
- If the asset is measured using a revaluation model then it should be revalued to fair value before being classified as held for sale.
- The asset will be presented as a current asset.
- No further depreciation is charged.

Exam focus

Exam Kit questions in this area:

- Renshu
- Bohai
- Jassie
- Luna
- Sterling
- Juan
- Cutherd
- Jobon
- Cial

chapter

6

Agriculture and Inventories

In this chapter

- IAS 41 *Agriculture.*
- IAS 2 *Inventories.*

IAS 41 *Agriculture*

Definition

A biological asset is a '**living plant or animal**' (IAS 41, para 5).

Agricultural produce is the '**harvested product of the entity's biological assets**' (IAS 41, para 5).

The key rules from the standard are:

- Biological assets are initially measured at fair value less estimated costs to sell.
- At each reporting date, biological assets are revalued to fair value less costs to sell.
- At the date of harvest, agricultural produce should be recognised and measured at fair value less estimated costs to sell. It is then accounted for under IAS 2 Inventories.

IAS 2 *Inventories*

Definition

Inventories are assets that the entity sells in the ordinary course of business (plus any raw materials and work in progress).

Inventories are measured at '**the lower of cost and net realisable value**' (IAS 2, para 9):

- **Cost** includes the purchase price and any other directly attributable costs.
- **Net realisable value** is the expected selling price, less estimated costs of completion and sale.

Exam focus

Exam Kit questions in this area:

- Fill
- Lucky Dairy

chapter

7

Foreign currency in individual financial statements

In this chapter

- Functional currency.
- Translation rules.

Functional currency

Definition

IAS 21 *The Effects of Changes in Foreign Exchange Rates* states that functional currency is '**the currency of the primary economic environment where an entity operates**' (IAS 21, para 8).

Factors used to determine a functional currency are as follows:

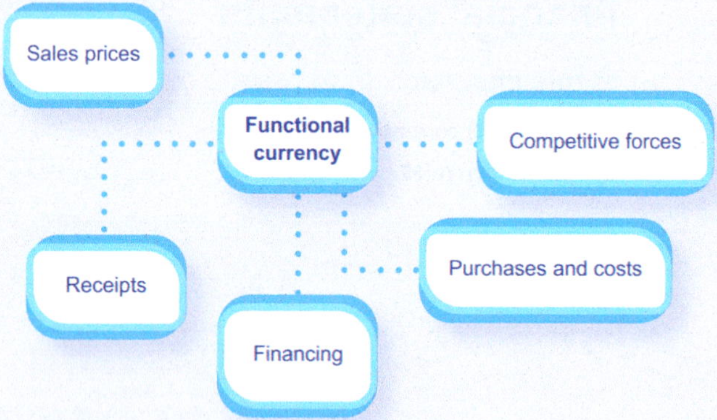

A subsidiary that operates with little autonomy will most likely have the same functional currency as its parent.

Translation rules

Overseas transactions

Initial transaction

Translate into functional currency using the spot/historic rate.

Settlement

Translate the settlement into functional currency using the spot/historic rate.

If unsettled

The treatment depends on whether the overseas item is monetary.

If monetary

E.g. receivables, payables, loans

Retranslate at the closing rate of exchange.

If non-monetary

E.g. PPE, inventories

Do not retranslate.

However, if held under a fair value model, the fair value will need to be translated when determined.

Presentation of exchange gains and losses

Exchange gains and losses should be presented in the same section of the statement of profit or loss as the related income and expenses.

Exam Focus

Exam Kit questions in this area:

- Rubul
- Peony
- Cial

chapter

8

Leases

In this chapter

- IFRS 16 *Leases.*
- Lessee accounting.
- Lessor accounting.
- Sale and leaseback.

IFRS 16 *Leases*

Definition

A **lease** is a contract that conveys the right to use an underlying asset for a period of time in exchange for consideration.

The **lessor** is the entity that provides the right-of-use asset and, in exchange, receives consideration.

The **lessee** is the entity that obtains use of the right-of-use asset and, in exchange, transfers consideration.

A **sublease** is a transaction for which an underlying asset is re-leased by a lessee ('intermediate lessor') to a third party. The original lease ('head lease') between the head lessor and lessee remains in effect.

Identifying a lease

A contract contains a lease if it conveys the right to control the use of an identified asset for a period of time in exchange for consideration. For this to be the case, the contract must give the customer:

- the right to substantially all of the economic benefits from use of the identified asset, and
- the right to direct the use of the identified asset.

Lessee accounting

Initial treatment

Except for the exceptions noted later, the lessee should recognise a lease liability and a right-of-use asset at the commencement of the lease:

Lease

Liability at present value of:

- Fixed payments
- Variable payments
- Residual value guarantees
- Purchase options*
- Termination penalties*

Right-of-use asset at total of:

- Initial liability value
- Payments at/before commencement
- Direct costs
- Dismantling costs

* Include if reasonably certain to be incurred.

Subsequent treatment

- The carrying amount of the lease liability is increased by the interest charge. This interest is also recorded in the statement of profit or loss (financing section). The carrying amount of the lease liability is reduced by cash repayments.
- The right-of-use asset is measured using the cost model (unless another measurement model is chosen). This means it is measured at its initial cost less accumulated depreciation and impairment losses.

Exceptions

The lessee can choose to recognise the lease payments in profit or loss on a straight line basis if the lease is

- short-term (less than 12 months at the inception date), or
- of a low value.

Lessor accounting

Lease classifications

Leases must be classified at inception as either a finance lease or an operating lease:

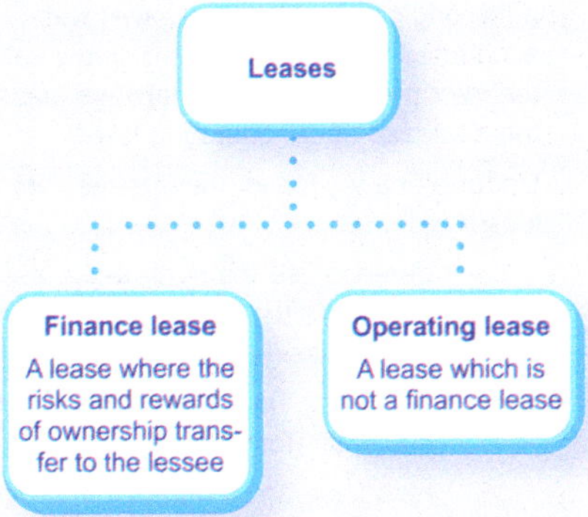

IFRS 16 gives the following indications that the risks and rewards of ownership have transferred to the lessee:

- Ownership is transferred at the end of the lease
- The lessee has the option to purchase the asset at the end of the lease term for less than fair value
- The lessee can continue to lease the asset at the end of the lease term for less than market rents
- The lease term is for the major part of the asset's life
- The present value of the minimum lease payments are substantially all of the fair value of the leased asset.

Lessor accounting treatment

Under a finance lease, the lessor must:

- derecognise the leased asset
- recognise a lease receivable at the present value of the minimum lease payments plus the estimated unguaranteed residual value of the asset
- recognise income on the lease receivable in the statement of profit or loss (investing section) using the rate implicit in the lease.

Under an operating lease, the lessor must:

- continue to recognise and depreciate the leased asset
- recognise lease rental income in profit or loss (operating section) on a straight line basis.

Subleases

The intermediate lessor must classify the sublease as an operating or finance lease but with reference to the right-of-use asset, not the underlying asset in the lease.

If the original lease (as a lessee) was accounted for as if short term or low value, the intermediate lessor will **always** classify the sublease as an operating lease.

Under a finance lease, the intermediate lessor will:

- derecognise the right-of-use asset relating to the head lease (for which it is the lessee)
- recognise the net investment in the sublease (for which it is a lessor)
- recognise any difference in profit or loss (operating section)
- retain the lease liability relating to the head lease in its statement of financial position.

Under an operating lease, the intermediate lessor will:

- retain the right-of-use asset and the lease liability relating to the head lease (for which it is the lessee)
- recognise a depreciation charge for the right-of-use asset and interest on the lease liability (as per lessee accounting)
- recognise lease income from the sublease.

Sale and leaseback

The treatment of a sale and leaseback depends on whether the 'sale' represents the satisfaction of a performance obligation (as per IFRS 15 *Revenue from Contracts with Customers*).

	Transfer is not a sale	**Transfer is a sale**
Seller-lessee	Continue to recognise asset. Recognise a financial liability equal to proceeds received.	Derecognise the asset. Recognise a right-of-use asset as the proportion of the previous carrying amount that relates to the rights retained. Recognise a lease liability. A profit or loss on disposal will arise (recorded in the operating section).
Buyer-lessor	Do not recognise the asset. Recognise a financial asset equal to transfer proceeds.	Account for the asset purchase. Account for the lease by applying lessor accounting requirements.

Exam focus

Exam Kit questions in this area:

- Bohai
- Benito

chapter

9

Employee benefits

In this chapter

- Overview.
- Pensions.
- Measurement of defined benefit pension assets and liabilities.
- Short-term and other long-term benefits.
- Termination benefits.

Overview

Exam focus

- Pension schemes are accounted for in accordance with IAS 19 *Employee Benefits.*
- You must be prepared to deal with computational and discussion elements.

Definition

Types of pension scheme

Defined contribution

An entity pays fixed contributions and will have no legal or constructive obligation to pay further contributions if the fund does not hold sufficient assets to pay all employee benefits.

Defined benefit

A pension scheme that is not a defined contribution scheme.

Pensions

For a defined contribution scheme, contributions payable are recognised as an expense in profit or loss (operating section).

The accounting treatment of a defined benefit scheme is covered in more detail in the next section.

Measurement of defined benefit pension assets and liabilities

IAS 19 requires that:

- **plan assets** are measured at their fair value at the end of the reporting period
- **plan liabilities** are measured on an actuarial basis and are discounted to present value at the end of the reporting period.

The net liability (deficit) or net asset (surplus) is reported at each reporting date.

Note that where there is a net asset, the **asset ceiling test** applies. This restricts the value of the net asset reported to the extent that it is regarded as recoverable.

Defined benefit plan movement

The following proforma shows the movement on the defined benefit deficit (or a surplus) over a reporting period:

	$
Net deficit/(asset) brought forward (Obligation b/f – assets b/f)	X/(X)
Net interest component	X/(X)
Service cost component	X
Contributions into plan	(X)
Benefits paid	–
	X/(X)
Remeasurement component (bal. fig)	X/(X)
Net deficit/(asset) carried forward (Obligation c/f – assets c/f)	X/(X)

Definitions

- **Current service cost** is the '**increase in the present value of the defined benefit obligation resulting from employee service in the current period**' (IAS 19, para 8). This is part of the service cost component, which is recorded in the statement of profit or loss (operating section).
- **Past service cost** is the '**change in present value of the defined benefit obligation for employee service in prior periods resulting from a plan amendment or curtailment in the current period**' (IAS 19, para 8). This is part of the service cost component.
- A **curtailment** arises when there is a significant reduction in the number of employees covered by a plan. Any gain or loss on curtailment is part of the service cost component.

- A **settlement** arises when an entity enters into a transaction to terminate all or part of the benefits due to one or more employees under a plan. This is part of the service cost component.
- **Net interest component** is the change in measurement in both the plan obligation and plan assets due to the passage of time. It is calculated by applying the discount rate for the liability to the net liability (or asset) at the start of the reporting period. This is charged (or credited) to profit or loss (financing section).
- **The remeasurement component** arises due to differences between assumptions and estimates made when accounting for the defined benefit plan, and what has actually happened. The remeasurement component is taken to other comprehensive income.

Plan amendments, curtailments and settlements

If there is a plan amendment, settlement or curtailment (PASC) then the effect of this is calculated by comparing the net defined benefit deficit before and after the event.

The Board have amended IAS 19 to clarify that the reporting entity must determine:

- the current service cost for the remainder of the reporting period after the PASC using the actuarial assumptions used to remeasure the net defined benefit liability
- net interest for the remainder of the reporting period after the PASC using the remeasured defined benefit deficit and the discount rate used to remeasure the defined benefit deficit.

Recognising the amounts in the financial statements

Defined benefit pension plan

Profit or loss

- Service cost component
- Net interest component

Other comprehensive income

- Remeasurement component

Statement of financial position

- Plan obligation
- Plan assets
- Asset ceiling

Short-term and other long-term benefits

Short-term benefits

This category includes items that will be settled within 12 months of the end of the reporting period when the employee provided the relevant service, such as wages and salaries. The costs are expensed as incurred in accordance with the accruals concept.

Other long-term benefits

This category includes items not expected to be settled within 12 months of the end of the reporting period when the employee provided the relevant service, such as deferred remuneration.

Other long-term benefits are accounted for in the same way as a defined benefit scheme, except that any remeasurement component is recorded in the statement of profit or loss (most likely within the operating section).

Termination benefits

Definition

Termination benefits are benefits payable as a result of employment being terminated, either by the employer, or by the employee accepting voluntary redundancy.

Recognition

The reporting entity recognises a liability and expense at the earlier of the date when:

- the entity can no longer withdraw the termination benefits offer
- the entity recognises restructuring costs in accordance with IAS 37 *Provisions, Contingent Liabilities and Contingent Assets.*

Measurement

Termination benefits are measured on initial recognition.

Subsequent measurement depends on the nature of the benefit (i.e. whether it is short-term, a pension enhancement, or another type of long-term benefit).

Exam focus

Exam Kit questions in this area:

- Columbia
- Layout

chapter

10

Share-based payment

In this chapter

- Overview.
- Accounting for share-based payments.
- Hybrid transactions.

Overview

IFRS 2 *Share-based Payment* applies where an entity receives goods or services in exchange for shares, share options or cash based on a share price.

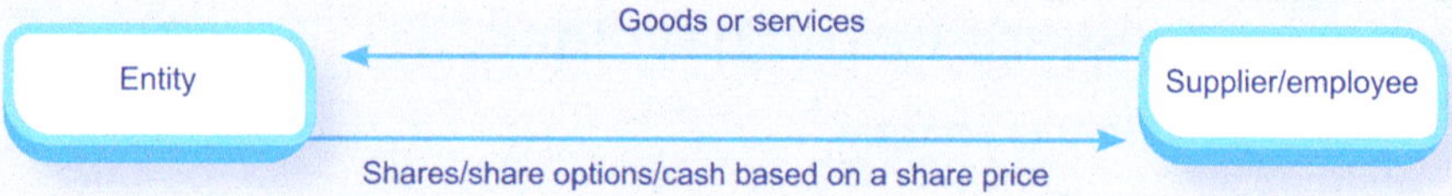

Recognising the transaction

The expense of a share-based payment scheme is accounted for over the vesting period based on the number of share-based payments expected to vest. If there are no vesting conditions, then the transaction is accounted for immediately.

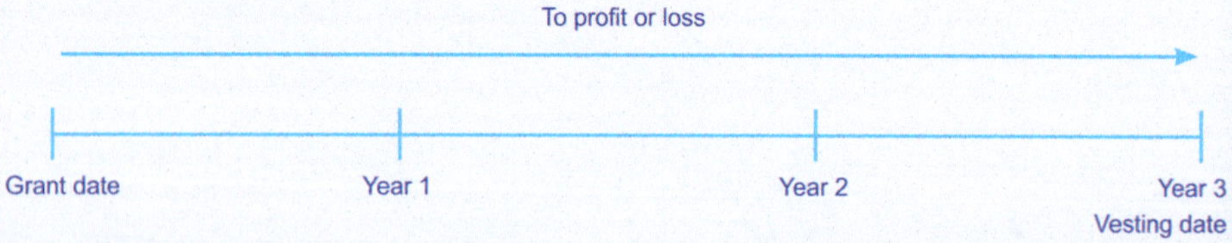

Definitions

Grant date: the date a share-based payment transaction is entered into.

Vesting date: the date on which the cash or equity instruments can be received by the other party to the agreement.

There are two types of share based payment transactions:

(1) **Equity-settled** share based payment transactions where a company receives goods or services in exchange for equity instruments (e.g. shares or share options).

(2) **Cash-settled** share based payment transactions, where a company receives goods and services in exchange for a cash amount paid based on its share price.

Accounting for share-based payments

Equity-settled share-based payments

The value of an equity-settled share-based payment transaction is determined as follows:

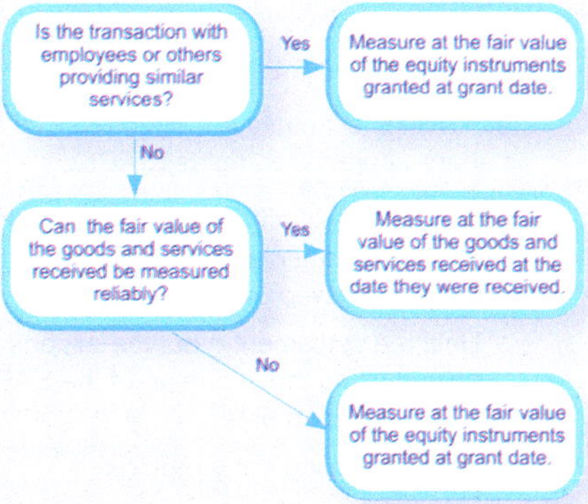

This should be recognised in profit or loss over the vesting period based on the number of shares or options that are expected to vest.

The accounting entry posted at each reporting date is:

Dr Profit or loss (operating section)

Cr Equity

Cash-settled share-based payments

Cash-settled schemes are often referred to as share-appreciation rights (SARs).

There are two key differences between the accounting treatment of SARs and an equity-settled share-based payment scheme:

- Until the settlement date, the expense is valued using the fair value of the SARs at the reporting date.
- The accounting entry required is:

  Dr Profit or loss (operating section)

  Cr Liabilities

Hybrid transactions

Entity choice

If a share-based payment transaction gives the entity a choice over whether to settle in cash or by issuing equity instruments, IFRS 2 states that:

- The scheme is treated as a cash-settled share-based payment transaction if the entity has an obligation to settle in cash.
- If no obligation exists to settle in cash, then it is treated as an equity-settled share-based payment scheme.

Counterparty choice

If the share-based payment transaction gives the counterparty the choice of settling in cash or in equity instruments then the credit entry is split between equity and liabilities:

- If the transaction is with employees, the equity element is calculated as the fair value of the equity alternative at the grant date less the fair value of the cash alternative at the grant date.
- If the transaction is not with employees, the equity element is calculated as the fair value of the good or service received, less the fair value of the cash alternative at the date of the transaction.
- The liability element is calculated by taking the cash settlement option and applying the rules for cash-settled share-based payments.

The equity and liability components will be recognised over the vesting period.

Exam focus

Exam Kit questions in this area:

- Luploid
- Symbal
- Kimimila

chapter

11

Provisions and events after the reporting period

In this chapter

- IAS 37 *Provisions, Contingent Liabilities and Contingent Assets.*
- IAS 10 *Events after the Reporting Period.*

IAS 37 *Provisions, Contingent Liabilities and Contingent Assets*

Definition

- A provision is '**a liability of uncertain timing or amount**' (IAS 37, para 10).
- A contingent liability is a possible obligation whose existence will be confirmed by uncertain future events outside of the entity's control.
- A contingent asset is a possible asset whose existence will be confirmed by uncertain future events outside of the entity's control.

Provisions

Recognition

Recognise when:

- an entity has a present obligation (legal or constructive) as a result of a past event,
- it is probable that an outflow of economic benefits will be required, and
- a reliable estimate can be made.

Measurement

- The amount recognised should be the **best estimate** of the expenditure required to settle the obligation.
- Where the time value of money is material, the provision should be discounted to present value.

Specific guidance

Future operating losses

- Provisions should not be recognised for future operating losses.

Onerous contracts

- Provisions should be recognised for the obligation under the contract.

Restructuring

- Provisions can only be recognised where an entity has a constructive obligation to carry out the restructuring.
- A constructive obligation arises when there is a detailed formal plan and the plan has been announced to those affected.
- A restructuring provision should only include the direct costs of restructuring.

Contingent liabilities should not be recognised. They should be disclosed unless the possibility of a transfer of economic benefits is remote.

Contingent assets should not be recognised. If the possibility of an inflow of economic benefits is probable they should be disclosed.

IAS 10 *Events after the Reporting Period*

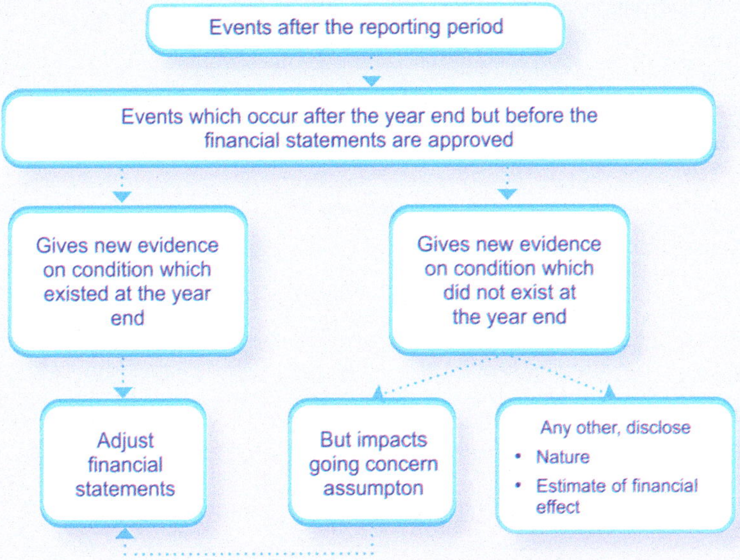

Exam focus

Exam Kit questions in this area:

- Rubul
- Wing
- Juan
- Jobon

chapter

12

Financial instruments

In this chapter

- Definitions.
- Financial liabilities.
- Compound financial instruments.
- Financial assets.
- Financial asset impairments.
- Derecognition of financial instruments.
- Derivatives.
- Hedge accounting.
- Disclosure of financial instruments.

Definitions

A financial instrument is '**any contract that gives rise to a financial asset of one entity and a financial liability or equity instrument of another entity**' (IAS 32, para 11).

A **financial asset** is any asset that is:

- '**cash**
- **an equity instrument of another entity**
- **a contractual right to receive cash or another financial asset from another entity**
- **a contractual right to exchange financial instruments with another entity under conditions that are potentially favourable**' (IAS 32, para 11).

A **financial liability** is any liability that is a:

- '**contractual obligation to deliver cash or another financial asset to another entity**
- **contractual obligation to exchange financial instruments with another entity under conditions that are potentially unfavourable**
- **a contract that will or may be settled in the entity's own equity instruments, and is a non-derivative for which the entity is or may be obliged to deliver a variable number of the entity's own equity instruments**' (IAS 32, para 11).

An **equity instrument** is '**any contract that evidences a residual interest in the assets of an entity after deducting all of its liabilities**' (IAS 32, para 11).

Financial instruments and the presentation of income and expenses

Accounting for financial instruments may lead to income and expenses being recognised in the statement of profit or loss. The income and expenses will typically be classified as follows:

- income and expenses related to financial assets are presented in the investing section
- income and expenses related to financial liabilities are presented in the financing section.

Note there are different rules for derivatives and hedging instruments.

For entities with a specified main business activity that involves investing or financing (e.g. hedge funds, banks), some income and expenses related to financial assets and liabilities may need to be presented in the operating section.

Financial liabilities

Initial recognition

At initial recognition, financial liabilities are measured at fair value.

- If the financial liability will be held at fair value through profit or loss, transaction costs should be expensed to the statement of profit or loss.
- If the financial liability will not be held at fair value through profit or loss, transaction costs should be deducted from its carrying amount.

Subsequent treatment

The subsequent treatment of a financial liability is that they can be measured at either:

- amortised cost
- fair value through profit or loss.

Amortised cost

This category is used for most financial liabilities.

Interest income is calculated using the effective rate. This is charged to profit or loss and increases the carrying amount of the financial liability. Cash payments reduce the liability's carrying amount.

Fair value through profit or loss

This category is used for derivatives or liabilities held for trading.

The financial liability is revalued to fair value at the reporting date with the gain or loss in profit or loss.

A designation can be made to use this category in order to reduce an accounting mismatch. In this instance, the change in the fair value of the liability must be split:

- the change due to own credit risk is reported in OCI
- the remaining change is reported in profi or loss.

Compound financial instruments

A compound instrument is a financial instrument that has characteristics of both equity and liabilities. An example would be debt that can be redeemed either in cash or a fixed number of equity shares.

IAS 32 requires issuers of compound instruments to split them into:

- a financial liability (the liability to repay the debt holder in cash)
- an equity instrument (the option to convert into shares).

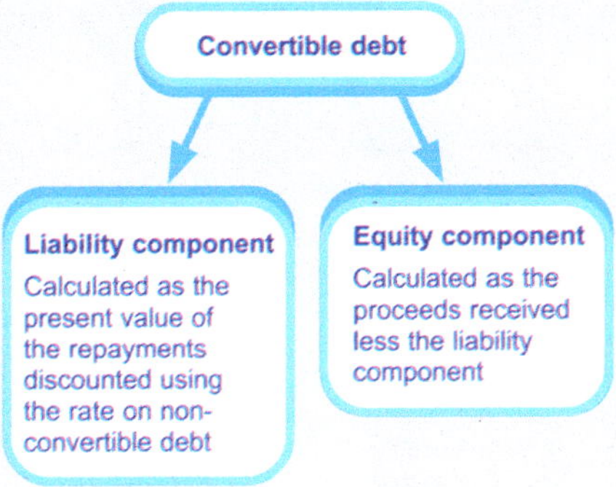

Financial assets

Initial recognition

At initial recognition, financial assets are measured at fair value.

- If the financial asset will be held at fair value through profit or loss, transaction costs should be expensed to the statement of profit or loss.
- If the financial asset will not be held at fair value through profit or loss, transaction costs should be added to its carrying amount.

Investments in equity

Investments in equity instruments (such as an investment in the ordinary shares of another entity) are normally measured at fair value through profit or loss.

It is possible to measure an equity instrument at fair value through other comprehensive income, provided that:

- the equity instrument is not held for trading, and
- an irrevocable choice for this designation is made upon initial recognition of the asset.

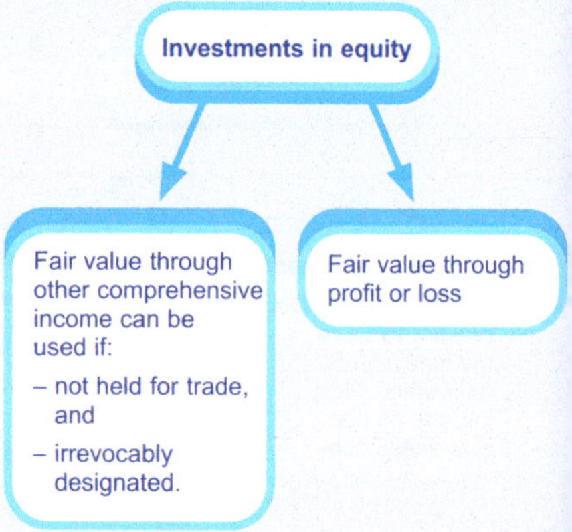

Investments in debt

Financial assets that are debt instruments can be measured in one of three ways:

1. An investment in a debt instrument is measured at **amortised cost** if:
   - The financial asset is held within a business model whose aim is to collect the contractual cash flows.
   - The contractual terms of the financial asset give rise to cash flows that are solely payments of principal and interest on the principal amount outstanding.
2. An investment in a debt instrument is measured at **fair value through other comprehensive income** if:
   - The financial asset is held within a business model whose objective is achieved by both collecting contractual cash flows and selling financial assets.
   - The contractual terms of the financial asset give rise to cash flows that are solely payments of principal and interest on the principal amount outstanding.
3. An investment in a debt instrument that is not measured at amortised cost or fair value through other comprehensive income will be measured at **fair value through profit or loss.**

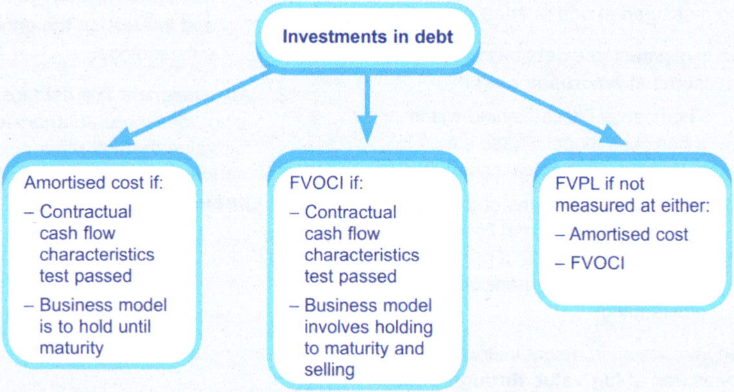
Investments in debt
Amortised cost if:
– Contractual cash flow characteristics test passed
– Business model is to hold until maturity
FVOCI if:
– Contractual cash flow characteristics test passed
– Business model involves holding to maturity and selling
FVPL if not measured at either:
– Amortised cost
– FVOCI

Financial asset impairments

The impairment rules in IFRS 9 apply to debt instruments measured at amortised cost or at fair value through other comprehensive income.

For financial assets within the scope of the impairment rules, entities must calculate a loss allowance.

Increases and decreases in the loss allowance are charged to profit or loss. The classification of the amount recognised in the profit or loss will depend on the nature of the business and the type of financial asset.

This loss allowance must be equal to:

- **12 month expected credit losses** if credit risk has not increased significantly.
- **Lifetime expected credit losses** if credit risk has increased significantly.

Definitions

Credit loss: the present value of the difference between the contractual cash flows due to an entity and the cash flows that it expects to receive.

Expected credit loss: the weighted average credit losses.

Lifetime expected credit losses: The expected credit losses that result from all possible default events.

12 month expected credit losses: The proportion of the lifetime expected credit losses that arise from default events within 12 months of the reporting date.

Derecognition of financial instruments

Key Point

A financial asset should be derecognised if one of the following has occurred:

- the contractual rights to the cash flows of the financial asset have expired.
- the financial asset has been sold and substantially all the **risks and rewards of ownership** have been transferred from the seller to the buyer.

A financial liability should be derecognised when the obligation specified in the contract is discharged, cancelled or has expired.

The accounting treatment of derecognition is as follows:

- The difference between the carrying amount of the asset or liability and the amount received or paid should be recognised in profit or loss for the period.
- For investments in equity instruments held at fair value through other comprehensive income, the cumulative gains and losses recognised in other comprehensive income are **not reclassified** to profit or loss on disposal.
- For investments in debt instruments held at fair value through other comprehensive income, the cumulative gains and losses recognised in other comprehensive income **are reclassified** to profit or loss on disposal.

Modification of debt

If the terms of an existing loan are changed, or it is exchanged for a new loan with the existing lender, the accounting treatment depends on whether the new terms are deemed to be substantially different.

- If the terms are **substantially different**, the original liability is derecognised and a new liability recognised at fair value. Any difference is recognised in profit or loss, alongside any fees incurred.
- If the terms are not **substantially different**, the original liability is restated to the present value of the revised cash flows, with any fees paid being deducted. Any difference is recognised in profit or loss.

Derivatives

Definitions

A derivative is a financial instrument with the following characteristics:

(a) Its value changes in response to an underlying variable.

(b) It requires little or no initial investment.

(c) It is settled at a future date.

Derivatives are measured at fair value through profit or loss.

Amounts recognised in the profit or loss would typically be classified in the operating section, unless the derivative relates to a transaction that involves only the raising of finance, in which case the amounts would be classified in the financing section.

Hedge accounting

Types of hedge accounting

A fair value hedge

'A hedge of the exposure to changes in fair value of a recognised asset or liability or an unrecognised firm commitment that is attributable to a particular risk and could affect profit or loss (or other comprehensive income for equity investments measured at fair value through other comprehensive income)' (IFRS 9, para 6.5.2).

A cash flow hedge

'A hedge of the exposure to variability in cash flows that is attributable to a particular risk associated with a recognised asset or liability or a highly probable forecast transaction and that could affect profit or loss' (IFRS 9, para 6.5.2).

Key Point

Derivatives introduce volatility into profit or loss. Hedge accounting is a method of managing this by designating one or more hedging instruments so that their change in fair value is offset, in whole or in part, by the change in fair value or cash flows of a hedged item.

Criteria

Under IFRS 9, hedge accounting rules can only be applied if the hedging relationship meets the following:

- The hedge consists of eligible hedging instruments and hedged items.
- At the inception of the hedge formal documentation identifies the hedged item and the hedging instrument.
- The hedging relationship is effective.

- If the hedged item is a forecast transaction, then the transaction must be highly probable.

A hedging relationship is effective if the following three criteria are met:

1. **'There is an economic relationship between the hedged item and the hedging instrument.**
2. **The effect of credit risk does not dominate the value changes that result from that economic relationship.**
3. **The hedge ratio of the hedging relationship is the same as that resulting from the quantity of the hedged item that the entity actually hedges and the quantity of the hedging instrument that the entity actually uses to hedge that quantity of hedged item'** (IFRS 9, para 6.4.1).

Accounting treatment of a fair value hedge

At the reporting date:

- the hedging instrument will be remeasured to fair value
- the carrying amount of the hedged item will be adjusted for the change in fair value since the inception of the hedge.

The gain (or loss) on the hedging instrument and the loss (or gain) on the hedged item will be recorded:

- in profit or loss in most cases, but
- in other comprehensive income if the hedged item is an investment in equity that is measured at fair value through other comprehensive income.

The gains and losses on both the hedging instrument and hedged item will typically be presented in the same section of profit or loss (determined by reference to the nature of the hedged item).

Accounting treatment of a cash flow hedge

For cash flow hedges, the hedging instrument will be remeasured to fair value at the reporting date.

- The gain or loss is recognised in other comprehensive income.
- However, if the gain or loss on the hedging instrument since the inception of the hedge is greater than the loss or gain on the hedged item then the **excess** gain or loss on the instrument must be recognised in profit or loss.
- Per IFRS 18, the excess gain on the hedging instrument is presented in the same section of profit or loss as the income and expenses affected by the hedged risk.

Discontinuing hedge accounting

An entity must cease hedge accounting if any of the following occur:

- The hedging instrument expires or is exercised, sold or terminated.
- The hedge no longer meets the hedging criteria.
- A forecast future transaction that qualified as a hedged item is no longer highly probable.

The discontinuance should be accounted for prospectively (entries posted to date are not reversed).

Disclosure of financial instruments

IFRS 7 *Financial Instruments: Disclosures* requires that entities disclose.

1. Information about the significance of financial instruments for an entity's financial position and performance.
2. Information about the nature and extent of risks arising from financial instruments.

Exam focus

Exam Kit questions in this area:

- Greer
- Fernanda
- Kabelo
- Jacinta
- Cial
- Kimimila
- Maple

chapter

13

Tax

In this chapter

- Introduction to taxation.
- Deferred tax.
- Calculating deferred tax.
- Accounting for deferred tax.
- Specific scenarios.

Introduction to taxation

There are two elements to tax that an entity has to deal with:

Current tax – the amount payable to the tax authorities in relation to the trading activities of the current period.

Deferred tax – an accounting measure used to match the tax effects of transactions with their accounting treatment.

In summary, the tax expense for an entity is calculated as follows:

Tax expense = current tax +/– movement in deferred tax.

Deferred tax

According to the accruals concept, the tax effect of a transaction should be reported in the same accounting period as the transaction itself.

Deferred tax is recognised on temporary differences between the accounting and tax treatment of a transaction.

IAS 12 Income Taxes states that a **temporary difference** is the difference between the carrying amount of an asset or liability and its tax base.

Examples of temporary differences include (but are not restricted to):

- Tax deductions for the cost of non-current assets that have a different pattern to the write off of the asset in the financial statements.
- Assets are revalued upwards in the financial statements, but no adjustment is made for tax purposes.
- Development costs are capitalised and amortised to profit or loss in future periods, but were deducted for tax purposes as incurred.

Calculating deferred tax

The first step is to determine the temporary differences:

- If the carrying amount exceeds the tax base, the temporary difference is said to be a taxable temporary difference (a liability).
- If the tax base exceeds the carrying amount, the temporary difference is a deductible temporary difference (an asset).

The tax rate in force (or expected to be in force) when the asset is realised or the liability is settled is applied to the temporary difference to calculate the deferred tax balance.

This rate must be based on legislation enacted or substantively enacted by the reporting date.

Deferred tax assets and liabilities are **not** discounted to present value.

Accounting for deferred tax

The entry to profit or loss and other comprehensive income in respect of deferred tax is the difference between the net liability/asset at the beginning of the year and the net liability/asset at the end of the year:

- If the item giving rise to the deferred tax is dealt with in profit or loss, the related deferred tax should also be presented in profit or loss.
- If the item giving rise to the deferred tax is dealt with in other comprehensive income, the related deferred tax should be recorded in other comprehensive income.

Specific scenarios

Share option schemes

The amount of tax relief granted is based on the intrinsic value of the options (the difference between the market price of the shares and the exercise price of the option) at the exercise date. This delayed tax relief gives rise to a deferred tax asset.

Unused tax losses

Where an entity has unused tax losses, IAS 12 allows a deferred tax asset to be recognised to the extent that it is probable that future taxable profits will be available against which the unused tax losses can be utilised.

Leases

If a lease transaction results in equal amounts of deductible and taxable temporary differences being created, then both a deferred tax asset and deferred tax liability should be recognised.

Business combinations

A business combination has deferred tax consequences:

- The identifiable net assets of the acquired subsidiary are consolidated at fair value but the tax base derives from the values in the subsidiary's individual financial statements. A temporary difference is created, giving rise to deferred tax in the consolidated financial statements.
- Provisions for unrealised profits reduce the carrying amount of inventory in the consolidated financial statements but the tax base is its cost in the individual financial statements. A temporary difference is created, giving rise to a deferred tax asset in the consolidated financial statements.

Goodwill itself does not give rise to deferred tax because IAS 12 specifically excludes it.

Exam focus

Exam Kit questions in this area:

- Chuckle
- Bohai
- Jobon
- Kimimila

chapter

14

Segment reporting

In this chapter

- IFRS 8 *Operating Segments.*

IFRS 8 Operating Segments

IFRS 8 Operating Segments requires a listed entity to disclose information about each of its operating segments.

Definition

An **operating segment** is a component of an entity:

- that engages in business activities
- whose operating results are regularly reviewed by the entity's chief operating decision maker
- that has discrete financial information available.

Aggregation

Two or more operating segments can be reported as a single operating segment provided that they have similar economic characteristics, and they are similar in terms of:

- the products or services they sell
- production processes
- types of customers
- distribution methods.

Reporting thresholds

An entity must separately report information about an operating segment that meets any of the following quantitative thresholds:

- **'its reported revenue, both sales to external customers and inter segment sales, is 10 per cent or more of the combined revenue of all operating segments.**

- **its reported profit or loss is 10 per cent or more of the greater, in absolute amount, of:**
  - **the combined reported profit of all operating segments that did not report a loss and**
  - **the combined reported loss of all operating segments that reported a loss.**
- **its assets are 10 per cent or more of the combined assets of all operating segments**' (IFRS 8, para 13).

At least 75% of the entity's external revenue should be included in reportable segments. This means that other segments might need to be identified as reportable segments until this 75% threshold is reached.

Disclosures

IFRS 8 requires detailed disclosures, including:

- factors used to identify the entity's reportable segments
- the types of products and services sold by each reportable segment.

For each reportable segment an entity should report:

- a measure of profit or loss
- a measure of total assets
- a measure of total liabilities (if this amount is used in decision making).

Benefits

Benefits of segmental reports include:

- enabling investors to view the business through the eyes of management
- improved transparency
- enabling investors to perform further analysis.

Limitations

Segmental reports have some limitations, including:

- distortion of segment results by trading between segments
- lack of comparability between entities
- potential for manipulation of segment definitions or performance measures
- cost allocation may be arbitrary.

Exam Focus

Exam Kit questions in this area:

- Eloa
- Dario

chapter

15

Related parties

In this chapter

- Related parties.
- Importance of related party disclosures.
- Related party disclosures.

Related parties

Exam Focus

- Related party transactions can affect the performance and position of an entity.
- In the exam you may have to determine related party transactions and the ethical implications of these.

Definition

IAS 24 *Related Party Disclosures* says that a person, or member of their close family, is related to the reporting entity if they:

- have control or joint control over the entity
- have significant influence over the reporting entity
- are a member of key management personnel of the entity or its parent.

Two entities are related if:

- they are parents and subsidiaries within the same group
- one entity is an associate or joint venture of the other
- a person (or a member of their close family) who is a related party of one of the entities has control over the other
- a person who has control over one of the entities also has significant influence over the other entity or is a member of its (or its parent's) key management personnel.

Summary

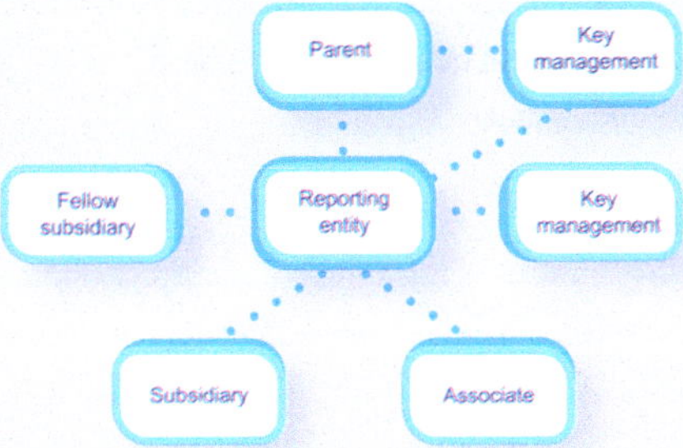

Definition

A **related party transaction** is the '**transfer of resources, services or obligations between related parties regardless of whether a price is charged**' (IAS 24, para 6).

Importance of related party disclosures

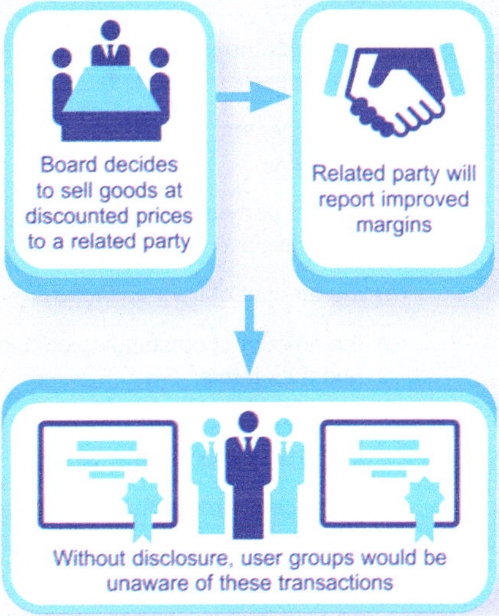

Related party disclosures

- Relationships between parents and subsidiaries.
- The name of the parent and the ultimate controlling party (if different).
- Key management personnel compensation.
- For related party transactions that have occurred disclosures should include:
  - (a) the amount of the transactions
  - (b) the amount of outstanding balances and their terms
  - (c) allowances for doubtful debts relating to the outstanding balances
  - (d) the expense recognised in the period in respect of irrecoverable or doubtful debts.

Exam Focus

Exam Kit questions in this area:

- Abasi

chapter

16

Adoption of International Financial Reporting Standards

In this chapter

- IFRS 1 *First-time Adoption of International Financial Reporting Standards.*
- Practical factors.

IFRS 1 *First-time Adoption of International Financial Reporting Standards*

This standard sets out the procedures to be followed in adopting IFRS Accounting Standards for the first time.

IFRS 1 defines the **date of transition** as the beginning of the earliest period for which an entity presents full comparative information in its first financial statements prepared under IFRS Accounting Standards.

1/1/X0
The date of transition to IFRS (The first day of the comparative period)

31/12/X0
Comparative figures for first set of published IFRS financial statements

31/12/X1
First set of published IFRS financial statements

Adoption of IFRS Accounting Standards

IFRS 1 states that the opening IFRS statement of financial position at the date of transition must:

- recognise all assets and liabilities required by IFRS Accounting Standards
- not recognise assets and liabilities not permitted by IFRS Accounting Standards
- reclassify all assets, liabilities and equity components in accordance with IFRS Accounting Standards
- measure all assets and liabilities in accordance with IFRS Accounting Standards.

Gains and losses arising on transition to IFRS Accounting Standards are recorded in retained earnings.

Practical factors

Before adopting a new set of accounting standards, an entity should consider the following:

- Bonuses and performance related pay – impact of profit changes?
- IT systems – will they require updating or replacing?
- Covenants on loans – will they be breached?
- Earnings per share – will it reduce?
- Perception – will analysts view the move positively?
- Staff knowledge – is it sufficient?

Exam focus

Exam Kit questions in this area:

- Whitebirk

chapter

17

Small and medium entities

In this chapter

- Small and medium-sized entities.
- The IFRS for SMEs Standard.

Small and medium sized entities

Definition

A small and medium sized entity (SME) is an entity that:

(1) does not have public accountability and

(2) publishes general purpose financial statements for external users.

The IFRS for SMEs Standard

Background

The IFRS for SMEs Standard was issued for use by entities that have no public accountability.

This standard reduces the burden of producing information that is not likely to be of interest to the stakeholders of a small or medium company.

Exam focus

The exam may ask you to discuss the differences between full IFRS Accounting Standards and the IFRS for SMEs Standard.

Omissions from the SMEs Standard

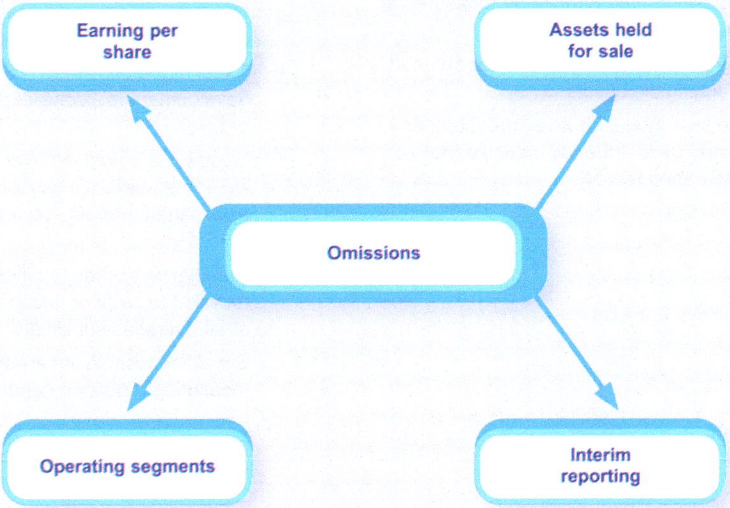

Disallowed treatments in the SMEs Standard

- The non-controlling interest at the acquisition date **cannot** be measured at fair value.
- The revaluation model **cannot** be used for intangible assets.
- The cost model for investment property is **only** used if the fair value cannot be determined reliably.

Simplifications in the SMEs Standard

- Borrowing costs are always expensed to profit or loss.
- Depreciation and amortisation methods do not need to be reviewed annually.
- Expenditure on research and development is always expensed to profit or loss.
- Goodwill is amortised over its useful life. If the useful life cannot be reliably established then an estimate of ten years or less should be used.
- Cumulative exchange differences are not recycled to profit or loss on the disposal of an overseas subsidiary.
- Simplified techniques are permitted when measuring a defined benefit obligation.

Exam focus

Exam Kit questions in this area:

- Handfood
- Whitebirk

chapter

18

Group accounting – basic groups

In this chapter

- Overview.
- IFRS 10 *Consolidated Financial Statements.*
- Business combinations.
- The acquisition method.
- Goodwill impairment.
- Basic workings.
- Associates.
- Joint arrangements.
- IFRS 12 *Disclosure of Interest in Other Entities.*
- IAS 27 *Separate Financial Statements.*
- IFRS 19 *Subsidiaries without Public Accountability: Disclosures.*

Overview

Exam focus

- Question one will always test group accounting. This question will include a pre-populated spreadsheet that contains a draft consolidated financial statement and one of the requirements will be to adjust this draft consolidated financial statement.
- In addition, a discussion of issues in the consolidated financial statements will also be required.

IFRS 10 *Consolidated Financial Statements*

Definition

A **parent** is an entity that controls another entity.

A **subsidiary** is an entity that is controlled by a parent entity.

IFRS 10 says that an investor has control when it has:

- power over the investee
- exposure, or rights to, variable returns from involvement in the investee
- the ability to use power over the investee to affect the investor's returns.

An entity that is a parent is required to produce consolidated financial statements.

Business combinations

IFRS 3 *Business Combinations* states that the acquisition method is used to account for business combinations.

Definition

A business combination is where an acquirer obtains control of a business.

Concentration test

An optional concentration test can be used to assess whether an acquired set of assets is **not** a business.

The acquired assets are not a business if substantially all of the fair value of the total assets acquired is concentrated in a single identifiable asset or group of similar identifiable assets.

Elements of a business

If the concentration test is not met, or if the test is not applied, a detailed assessment is required to assess if a business has been acquired.

To meet the definition of a business, inputs and substantive processes must have been acquired that can contribute to the creation of outputs.

Definition

Inputs are economic resources that can create outputs once processes are applied.

Processes are systems, standards or rules that can create outputs when applied to inputs.

Outputs include goods, services and income.

The acquisition method

The acquisition method has four requirements.

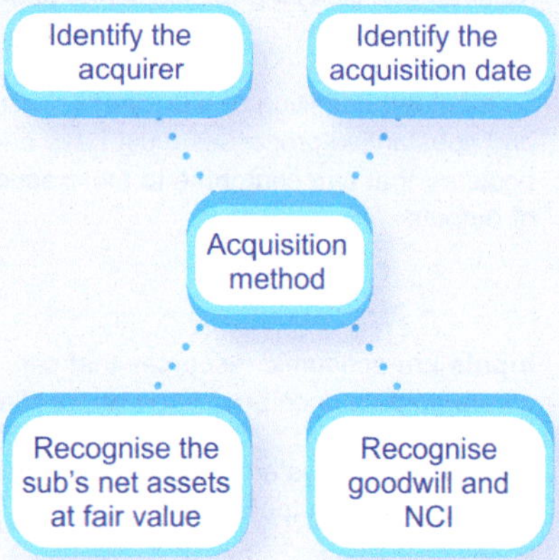

Identify the acquirer

The acquirer is the entity that has assumed control over another entity.

The acquirer is **normally** the company that has **transferred cash**, other assets or **shares** in the business combination.

Other factors to consider include:

- which entity's former management dominates the combined entity?
- which entity's former owners have the greatest number of votes in the combined entity?
- which entity was bigger?

Identify the acquisition date

This is the date on which the parent obtained control over the subsidiary.

Recognise the net assets

The acquirer must measure the identifiable assets acquired and the liabilities assumed at their **fair values** at the acquisition date.

Recognise goodwill and the NCI

When calculating goodwill, **purchase consideration** is measured at **fair value**.

Professional fees are **expensed** to profit or loss, most likely in the operating section.

The non-controlling interest at acquisition can either be measured:

- at **fair value** – this calculates full goodwill (P's goodwill + NCI's goodwill)
- its **proportionate share** of the fair value of the subsidiary's identifiable net assets – this calculates P's goodwill only.

Goodwill impairment

Goodwill is tested annually for impairment.

Goodwill does not generate independent cash flows and so is tested for impairment as part of a **cash-generating unit**. For exam purposes, this is normally a subsidiary.

Definition

A cash-generating unit is the smallest group of assets that generate cash inflows that are independent from other cash inflows in the business.

Key Point

Whether the NCI at acquisition was measured at fair value or proportionately has a significant impact on the impairment review:

- **Fair value method** – the group has recognised full goodwill so this can be added together with the other net assets of the subsidiary and compared with the recoverable amount.
- **Proportionate method** – only the group's share of goodwill has been recognised, so goodwill must be grossed up to include the NCI's share prior to performing the impairment review.

Basic workings

The SBR exam will ask you to adjust a draft financial statement, rather than prepare full consolidated financial statements. However, you may still need to use some of the following workings when adjusting a draft statement.

Consolidated statement of financial position	**$000**
Goodwill (W3)	X
Assets (P + S)	X
Total assets	X
Share capital (P's only)	X
Other components of equity (W5)	X
Retained earnings (W5)	X
NCI (W4)	X
Total equity	X
Liabilities (P + S)	X
Total equity and liabilities	X

Consolidated statement of financial position workings:

W1 Group structure

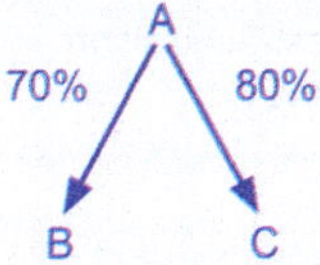

W2 Net assets of each subsidiary

	At acquisition date	At reporting date
	$000	$000
Equity share capital	X	X
Other components of equity	X	X
Retained earnings	X	X
Fair value adjustments	X /(X)	X /(X)
Post-acq'n accounting adjustments		
e.g. PURP on sales made by S		X /(X)
	X	X
	To W3	

W3 Goodwill

	$000
FV of consideration	X
NCI at acquisition	X
	X
FV of net assets at acquisition (W2)	(X)
Goodwill at acquisition	X
Impairment to date	(X)
Goodwill at reporting date	X

W4 Non-controlling interest

	$000
NCI at acquisition (W3)	X
NCI% x post-acquisition reserves (W2)	X
Less: NCI% of goodwill impairment (W3) (FV method only)	(X)
	X

W5 Group reserves

Retained earnings

	$000
Parent company (100%)	X
Subsidiary: Group share of post acquisition retained earnings (W2)	X
Less goodwill impairment (W3)*	(X)
PURP if P is seller	(X)
	X

*P% only if FV method used

Other components of equity

	$000
Parent company	X
Subsidiary: Group share of post-acquisition other components of equity (W2)	X
	X

Consolidated statement of profit or loss and other comprehensive income

Step 1: Identify the group structure

Step 2: Review the draft proforma

	$000
Revenue (P + S)	X
Cost of sales (P + S)	(X)
Gross profit	X
Operating costs (P + S)	(X)
Operating profit	X
Investment income (P + S)	X
Profit before financing and income taxes	X
Interest expense (P + S)	(X)
Profit before tax	X
Tax (P + S)	(X)
Profit for the period	Y
Other comprehensive income (P + S)	X
Total comprehensive income (TCI)	Z
Profit attributable to:	
Equity holders of group (bal.)	X
Non-controlling interest (step 4)	X
	Y
TCI attributable to:	
Equity holders of group (bal.)	X
Non-controlling interest (step 4)	X
	Z

Step 3: Adjust the proforma for errors or missing adjustments

This may include adjustments for the following:

- If the subsidiary has been acquired mid-year, confirm that the results of the subsidiary have been pro-rated so that only post-acquisition income, expenses and other comprehensive income are consolidated.
- Eliminate any intra-group income and expenses, unrealised profits on intra-group transactions, as well as any dividends received from the subsidiary that have not been adjusted for in the draft consolidated statement of profit or loss.

Step 4: Calculate or adjust the profit/TCI attributable to the non-controlling interest if relevant to the requirement

	Profit	TCI
	$000	$000
Profit/TCI of the subsidiary for the year (pro-rated for mid-year acquisition)	X	X
PURP (if S is the seller)	(X)	(X)
Excess depreciation/amortisation	(X)	(X)
Goodwill impairment (under FV model only)	(X)	(X)
	–––	–––
× NCI %	X	X
	–––	–––
Profit/TCI attributable to the NCI	X	X

Associates

Definition

- IAS 28 *Investments in Associates and Joint Ventures* defines an associate as **'an entity over which the investor has significant influence'** (IAS 28, para 3).
- Significant influence is the power to participate in the financial and operating policy decisions of an entity.
- A holding of between 20% and 50% of the voting power is presumed to give significant influence.

Accounting for associates

Associates are accounted for using the equity method.

Statement of financial position

	$000
Cost	X
Add: share of increase in net assets	X
Less: impairment losses	(X)
Investment in Associate	X

Profit or loss

Include the group's share of the associate's **profit after tax less any impairment losses** in the investing section of the consolidated statement of profit or loss.

Joint arrangements

Definition

Joint arrangements are defined in IFRS 11 *Joint Arrangements* as arrangements where '**two or more parties have joint control**' (IFRS 11, para 4). This exists when the relevant activities require unanimous consent of the parties that share control.

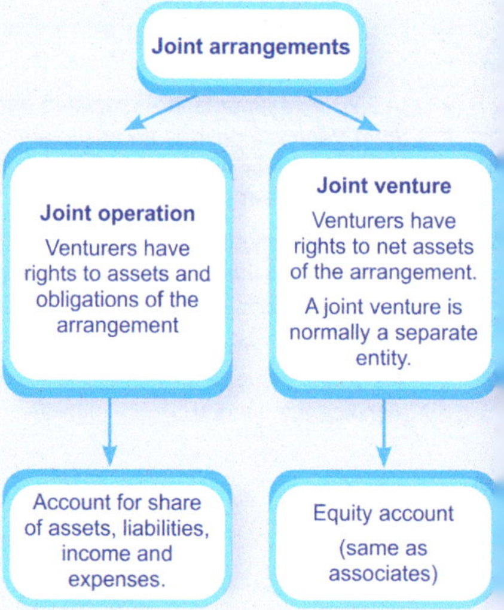

IFRS 12 *Disclosure of Interest in Other Entities*

IFRS 12 outlines the disclosures required when one entity has an investment in another.

IAS 27 *Separate Financial Statements*

IAS 27 applies when an entity has interests in subsidiaries, joint ventures or associates and it prepares separate non-consolidated financial statements.

In separate financial statements, investments in subsidiaries, joint ventures or associates can be accounted for in one of the following ways:

- cost
- in accordance with IFRS 9 Financial Instruments, or
- using the equity method.

IFRS 19 *Subsidiaries without Public Accountability: Disclosures*

Per IFRS 19, subsidiaries can apply IFRS 19 if they:

- do not have public accountability, and
- the ultimate parent entity produces consolidated financial statements that comply with IFRS Accounting Standards and which are available to the public.

By applying IFRS 19, subsidiaries will still follow the recognition, measurement and presentation requirements of other IFRS Accounting Standards, but the **disclosure requirements** will be those under IFRS 19, which have been **reduced**.

Exam focus

Exam Kit questions in this area:

- Sterling
- Luna
- Renshu
- Greer
- Eloa
- Peony
- Layout

chapter

19

Change in a group structure

In this chapter

- Overview.
- Step acquisition.
- Disposal of subsidiaries where control is lost.
- Presentation of disposal.
- Control to control scenarios.

Overview

This chapter concerns the impact of different types of share purchases and share sales on the consolidated financial statements.

Step acquisition

A step acquisition occurs when the parent company acquires control over the subsidiary in stages. Acquisition accounting is only applied at the date when control is achieved.

At the date control is achieved:

(1) re-measure the previously held equity interest to fair value

(2) recognise any resulting gain or loss in profit or loss for the year in the investing section (or in OCI if the shares were FVOCI)

(3) calculate goodwill and the non-controlling interest.

For the purposes of the goodwill calculation, use the following proforma:

	$000
Fair value of previously held interest	X
Fair value of consideration for additional interest	X
NCI at acquisition	X
	——
	X
Less: FV of net assets at acquisition	(X)
	——
Goodwill at acquisition	X
	——

Disposal of subsidiaries where control is lost

If the sale of shares causes control over a subsidiary to be lost, then the treatment in the consolidated financial statements is as follows:

- Consolidate the income and expenses of the subsidiary up until the disposal date.
- On disposal of the subsidiary, derecognise its assets, liabilities, goodwill and non-controlling interest and calculate a profit or loss on disposal (presented in the operating section of the consolidated statement of profit or loss).
- Recognise any remaining investment in the shares of the former subsidiary at fair value and subsequently account for this under the relevant accounting standard.
  - A holding of 20-50% of the shares would probably mean that the remaining investment is an associate, which should be accounted for using the equity method.
  - A holding of less than 20% of the shares would probably mean that the remaining investment should be accounted for under IFRS 9 Financial Instruments.

The profit or loss on disposal is calculated as follows:

	$000	$000
Disposal proceeds		X
Fair value of retained interest		X
		——
		X
Less interest in subsidiary disposed of:		
Net assets of subsidiary at disposal date	X	
Goodwill at disposal date	X	
Less: Carrying amount of NCI at disposal date	(X)	
	——	
		(X)
		——
Profit/(loss) to the group		X/(X)
		——

Presentation of disposal

If a subsidiary is acquired exclusively with a view to subsequent disposal and it meets the held for sale criteria in IFRS 5:

- it is presented in the financial statements as a disposal group classified as held for sale. This is achieved by amalgamating all its assets into one line item and all its liabilities into another
- it is measured, both on acquisition and at subsequent reporting dates, at fair value less costs to sell.

Control to control scenarios

Share purchases

Some share purchases simply increase the parent's holding in a subsidiary.

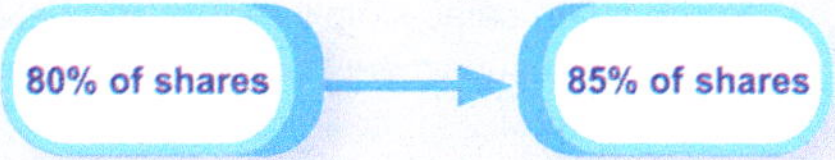

In such instances:

- Goodwill is **not** recalculated.
- A profit or loss **does not** arise in the consolidated financial statements.

The entry in the consolidated financial statements is:

Dr Non-controlling interest	X
Cr Cash	X
Dr/Cr Other components of equity	X (bal. fig.)

The decrease in NCI is calculated as the proportionate reduction in its carrying amount at the date of the group's additional purchase of shares.

Share sales

Some share sales simply reduce the parent's holding in a subsidiary but do not lead to a loss of control.

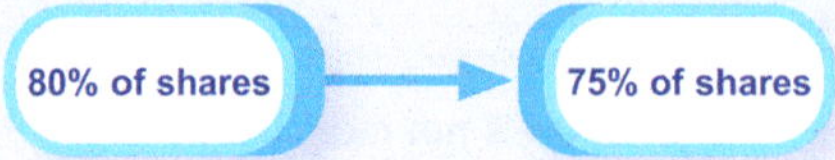

In such instances:

- Goodwill is **not** recalculated.
- A profit or loss **does not** arise in the consolidated financial statements.

The entry in the consolidated financial statements is:

Dr Cash	X
Cr Non-controlling interest	X
Dr/Cr Other components of equity	X (bal. fig.)

The increase in the NCI will be the share of the net assets (always) and goodwill (fair value method only) of the subsidiary at the date of disposal which the parent has effectively sold to the NCI.

Exam focus

Exam Kit questions in this area:

- Luna
- Sterling
- Greer

chapter

20

Group accounting – foreign currency

In this chapter

- Foreign subsidiaries.
- Proformas.
- Other foreign operations.

Foreign subsidiaries

If a company has foreign subsidiaries whose functional currency is their local currency, their financial statements must be translated into the parent's presentation currency.

- All **assets and liabilities** are translated into the group's presentation currency using the **closing rate** of exchange.
- **Goodwill** is treated as an asset of the subsidiary. It is calculated using the functional currency of the subsidiary. It is then translated using the closing rate for inclusion in the group accounts.
- **Income and expenses** must be translated at the average rate for the period.
- **Exchange differences** arising on consolidation are recognised in other comprehensive income. On disposal of the subsidiary, they are recycled to the statement of profit or loss.
- Exchange differences arise from:
  - the retranslation of the opening net assets using the closing rate
  - retranslation of the the profit for the year from the average rate (used in the statement of profit or loss) to the closing rate (for inclusion in the statement of financial position)
  - the retranslation of goodwill at each reporting date using the closing rate.

Proformas

Opening net assets and profit

The exchange gains or losses arising on the translation of opening net assets and profit for the year are generally calculated together.

The proforma for calculating the current year exchange gain or loss on the translation of the opening net assets and profit is as follows:

	DN	Exchange Rate	$
Opening net assets	X	Opening rate	X
Profit/(loss) for the year	X/(X)	Average rate	X/(X)
Exchange gain/(loss)	–	**Bal fig.**	X/(X)
Closing net assets	X	Closing rate	X

Goodwill translation

The proforma for calculating the current year exchange gain or loss on the retranslation of goodwill is as follows:

	DN	Exchange Rate	$
Opening goodwill	X	Opening rate	X
Impairment loss in year	(X)	Average rate	(X)
Exchange gain/(loss)	–	**Bal fig.**	X/(X)
Closing goodwill	X	Closing rate	X

Other foreign operations

The rules covered in this chapter also apply to the translation of overseas associates and joint arrangements.

Remember that:

- **Income, expenses and other comprehensive income** are translated at the exchange rate in place at the date of each transaction. The average rate for the year may be used as an approximation.
- **Assets and liabilities** are translated at the closing rate of exchange.
- **Exchange gains and losses** are recognised in other comprehensive income.

Exam focus

Exam Kit questions in this area:

- Peony

chapter

21

Group statement of cash flows

In this chapter

- Overview.
- Format of the statement of cash flows.
- Cash from operating activities before income taxes.
- Acquisitions and disposals.
- Dividends from associates.
- Dividends paid to non-controlling interests.

Overview

Key Point

- A statement of cash flows enables users of the financial statements to assess the **liquidity**, **solvency** and **financial adaptability** of a business.

Definition

- **Cash consists of** cash in hand and deposits repayable upon demand less overdrafts. This includes cash held in a foreign currency.
- **Cash equivalents** are '**short term, highly liquid investments that are readily convertible to known amounts of cash and are subject to an insignificant risk of changes in value**' (IAS 7, para 6).

Format of the statement of cash flows

IAS 7 *Statement of Cash Flows* requires that the statement is split into three sections – operating, investing and financing.

In the SBR exam you may be asked to adjust draft extracts from a consolidated statement of cash flows.

DEF Group statement of cash flows for the year ended 31 December 20X6

	$000	$000
Cash flows from operating activities		
Operating profit	X	
Adjustments for:		
Depreciation	X	
Impairment	X	
Profit on sale of non-current assets	(X)	
Increase in inventories	(X)	
Increase in receivables	(X)	
Increase in payables	X	
Cash from operating activities before income taxes		X
Income tax paid	(X)	
Net cash inflow from operating activities		X
Cash flows from investing activities		
Dividends received from associate	X	
Interest received	X	
Purchase of property, plant and equipment	(X)	
Proceeds from sale of property	X	
Acquisition of subsidiary, net of cash acquired	(X)	
Net cash used in investing activities		(X)

Cash flows from financing activities

Issue of ordinary share capital	X	
Repayment of loan	(X)	
Interest paid	(X)	
Dividends paid to NCI	(X)	
Dividends paid to parent shareholders	(X)	
Net cash used in financing activities		(X)
Net increase in cash and cash equivalents		X
Cash and cash equivalents brought forward		X
Cash and cash equivalents carried forward		X

Cash from operating activities before income taxes

IAS 7 allows 'cash from operating activities before income taxes' to be presented in one of two ways:

- **The indirect method** – this starts with operating profit and adjusts it to remove the effect of non-cash transactions and transactions (as per the proforma in the previous section).
- **The direct method** – this shows operating cash receipts and payments, such as cash receipts from customers, cash payments to suppliers, and cash payments to employees.

IAS 7 encourages the use of the direct method.

Acquisitions and disposals

The figure shown in the statement of cash flows is the net figure of two items.

- The cash spent on the purchase or received on the sale of the subsidiary.
- The cash balances (or overdraft). acquired or disposed of with a subsidiary.

The impact of subsidiary acquisitions and disposals will need to be factored into your workings throughout.

Dividends from associates

To find the dividend reconcile the opening and closing balance of the investment in the associate.

	$000
Associate b/f	X
Share of profit and OCI	X
Cash dividend received (**bal fig**)	(X)
Purchase of associates	X
Disposal of associates	(X)
Associate c/f	X

Dividends paid to non-controlling interests

Reconcile the opening to closing balance and the cash dividend paid is the balancing figure.

	$000
NCI b/f	X
Add: NCI on sub acquisition	X
Add: NCI share of profit and OCI	X
Less: NCI on sub disposal	(X)
Cash dividend paid (bal. fig)	(X)
NCI c/f	X

Exam focus

Exam Kit questions in this area:

- Fernanda
- Kabelo
- Apaniiwa

chapter

22

Analysis and Interpretation

In this chapter

- Purpose of financial reporting.
- Financial performance measures.
- Earnings per share.
- Additional performance measures.
- Non-financial information.
- Sustainability.
- Management commentary.

Exam Focus

Analysis and interpretation of information will always feature in Section B of the SBR exam.

Two professional marks will be available in this question.

Purpose of financial reporting

The purpose of financial reporting is to provide user groups with information that will help them to make decisions about providing resources to an entity.

Key user groups include:

- investors
- lenders
- other creditors, such as suppliers.

According to the Conceptual Framework, these users need information to assess:

- the entity's future cash flows
- management's stewardship of assets.

Financial performance measures

Calculating ratios helps users to understand an entity's financial performance and position and so can help users make investment decisions.

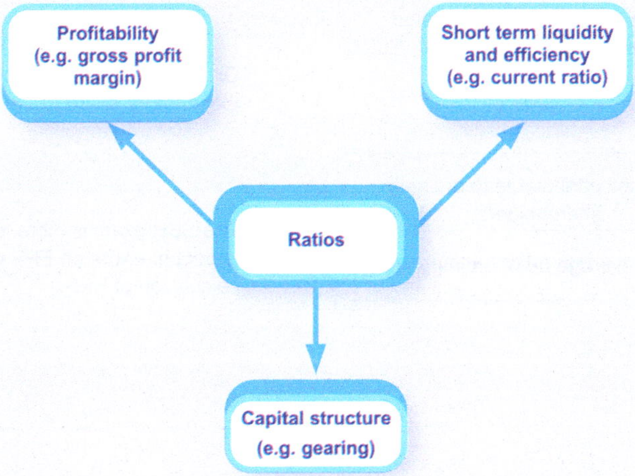

Earnings per share

Key Point

Earnings per share (EPS) is a ratio used to assess financial performance. In accordance with IAS 33 *Earnings per Share*, listed companies must disclose basic and diluted EPS.

Basic EPS

$$\frac{\text{Earnings attributable to ordinary shareholders}}{\text{Weighted average no.of ordinary shares}}$$

Diluted EPS

At the year end, an entity may have a commitment to issue more ordinary shares. Such commitments include:

- convertible loans
- share options.

Diluted EPS is an estimate of the impact of these future share issues on an entity's EPS

Exam Focus

The SBR exam is more likely to focus on the impact of errors on EPS rather than on the calculation of EPS.

Additional performance measures

Definition

Additional performance measures (APMs) are measures of performance not defined within IFRS Accounting Standards.

Types

Common APMs disclosed by entities include:

- **EBITDA** – earnings before interest, tax, depreciation and amortisation
- **Free cash flow** – cash flows from operating activities less capital expenditure.

Benefits

Benefits of disclosing APMs include:

- helping users to evaluate an entity through the eyes of management
- stripping out transactions that are not relevant to current or future year operating performance.

Drawbacks

APM disclosures have been criticised for:

- presenting an over-optimistic picture of the entity's performance
- giving undue prominence to figures that are not calculated in accordance with IFRS Accounting Standards.

MPMs and APMs

Some APMs will also meet the definition of a management-defined performance measure (MPM).

If an entity wants to publish an APM that meets the definition of an MPM, the entity will need to provide the disclosures required by IFRS 18 *Presentation and Disclosure in Financial Statements.*

Non-financial information

Criticisms of financial reporting

Financial performance measures:

- provide limited information about future performance
- do not provide information about key issues that impact long-term success, such as customer satisfaction
- can be manipulated through accounting estimates or policy choices.

Non-financial reporting measures

These are related to entity performance but are not expressed in monetary units. Examples include

- Employee turnover
- Customer satisfaction
- Delivery times

Sustainability

Goals

Sustainable Development Goals (SDGs) comprise 17 goals agreed by UN member states that include no poverty, zero hunger, reduced inequalities, and responsible production and consumption. They are only achievable through the cooperation of industry.

Companies should set sustainable development goals because:

- It is ethical
- Government funding will increasingly focus on sustainable businesses
- It reduces reputational and regulatory risk
- Sustainable products and services are a growth area
- Short-term, profit-based models are now less relevant for many investors.

Many investors are interested in companies that contribute to SDGs. Some will not invest in companies with low levels of pay or high levels of gender inequality.

Effective sustainability reporting provides useful information to potential and current investors because it helps them to make economic decisions about whether or not to advance financial resources to the reporting entity.

Reporting Standards

There are many reporting initiatives that can be used to communicate progress towards SDGs:

- The United Nations Global Compact (UNGC)
- The Global Reporting Initiative (GRI)
- The International Integrated Reporting Framework
- The International Sustainability Standards Board (ISSB).

Developments in sustainability reporting

The problem

The IFRS Foundation has publicly recognised the importance of sustainability reporting for an entity's stakeholders. For example:

- **Investors** want more information about climate risks in order to inform their decision making.
- **Banks** are focussing on climate-related risks when assessing financial stability.

Many sets of sustainability standards already exist. This causes significant diversity in how entities report sustainability issues.

The International Sustainability Standards Board

To overcome this problem, the IFRS Foundation formed a new board in 2021, called the International Sustainability Standards Board (ISSB).

The ISSB's aim is to develop a global set of sustainability reporting standards with the aim of harmonising and streamlining reporting in this area.

In 2023, the first ISSB standards, IFRS S1 *General requirements for disclosure of sustainability related financial information* and IFRS S2® *Climate-related disclosures*, were issued.

The IFRS Sustainability Standards can be adopted by any listed or private company on a voluntary basis but there is no mandate to apply the standards.

IFRS S1 *General requirements for disclosure of sustainability related financial information*

The objective of IFRS S1 is to **'require an entity to disclose information about its sustainability related risks and opportunities that is useful to primary users of general purpose financial reports in making decisions relating to providing resources to the entity.'** (IFRS S1, para 1)

Scope

- Entities should disclose information about all material sustainability related risks and opportunities that could reasonably be expected to affect the prospects of the entity.
- Disclosures should be included within general-purpose financial reports.
- IFRS S1 provides a global baseline for disclosures. However, entities can include disclosures that exceed this baseline.

Content

Per IFRS S1, an entity should provide disclosures that cover 4 sustainability related areas:

- governance
- strategy
- risk management
- metrics.

Judgements, uncertainties and errors

Judgements

- An entity will need to disclose information about the judgements it has made when preparing its sustainability related financial disclosures.

Uncertainties

- An entity will need to provide disclosures about the most significant uncertainties that affect amounts reported in the sustainability related financial disclosures.
- As far as possible, entities should be using data and assumptions that are consistent with those used in the financial statements.

Errors

- Material prior period errors will need to be corrected by restating the comparative amounts for the prior period(s) unless it is not possible to do so.

IFRS S2 *Climate-related disclosures*

IFRS S2 specifically applies to the disclosure of **climate-related** risks and opportunities.

IFRS S2 *Climate-related Disclosures'* objective is to **'require an entity to disclose information about its climate-related risks and opportunities that are useful to primary users of general purpose financial reports in making decisions relating to providing resources to the entity.'** (IFRS S2, para 1)

Scope

IFRS S2 applies to:

- climate-related risks to which the entity is exposed, which are:
  (i) **climate-related physical risks**
  (ii) **climate-related transition risks**
- **climate-related opportunities** available to the entity.

(IFRS S2, para 3)

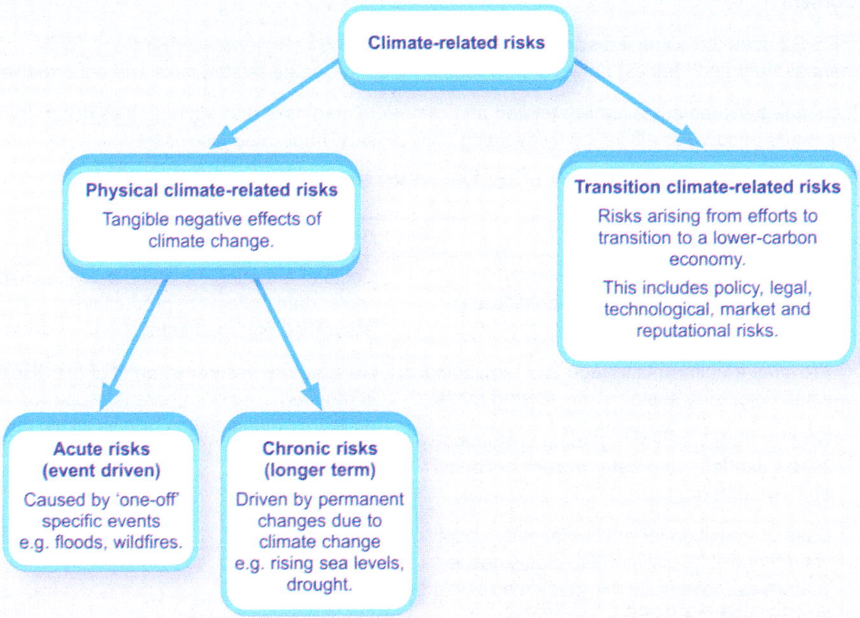
Climate-related risks
Physical climate-related risks
Tangible negative effects of climate change.
Transition climate-related risks
Risks arising from efforts to transition to a lower-carbon economy.
This includes policy, legal, technological, market and reputational risks.
Acute risks (event driven)
Caused by 'one-off' specific events e.g. floods, wildfires.
Chronic risks (longer term)
Driven by permanent changes due to climate change e.g. rising sea levels, drought.

Content

IFRS S2 uses the same 4 disclosure categories as IFRS S1 (Governance, Strategy, Risk management and Metrics) however now focussing upon climate-related risks and opportunities.

If overlap between sustainability related and climate related risks and opportunities occur, the standards encourage efficiency by avoiding unnecessary, duplicated disclosures.

Advantages and disadvantages of applying IFRS S1 and S2

Advantages	Disadvantages
Improves comparability of disclosures regarding sustainability between different entities.	Costs of adopting the standards – recruitment costs, data collection, production of reports, assurance engagements.
Provides a uniform language and terminologies when disclosing sustainability related matters.	No statutory assurance/audit of the disclosures is required, meaning there is scope for omission, manipulation or bias within the disclosure.
Greater transparency regarding sustainability issues can lead to greater access to capital and investment.	
Ease of transition for entities already adopting voluntary disclosure as IFRS Sustainability Standards incorporate the guidance utilised by the GRI and the SASB's Standards.	

European Sustainability Reporting Standards (ESRS)

For the SBR exam, knowledge of the differences between IFRS Sustainability Disclosure Standards and ESRS is required for the following areas:

	IFRS Sustainability Disclosure Standards	**ESRSs**
Enforceability	Voluntary basis unless jurisdiction authorities decide to require application	Mandatory for all companies already subject to a reporting obligation under the NFRD
Effective date	From 2024 (first reports in 2025)	From 2024 (first reports in 2025) for EU large Public Interest Entities and large non-EU companies listed on an EU market. All other EU entities (e,g. SMEs) progressively after 2025
Scope	Suitable for all profit-orientated and public sector entities	Large EU entities, large non-EU entities listed on an EU market and EU SMEs
Target users	Investors, lenders and creditors	Wider range of users

Coverage	There are two ISSB Standards: IFRS S1 *General Requirements for Disclosure of Sustainability-related Financial Information,* and IFRS S2 *Climate-related Disclosures*	There are 12 ESRS – Two cross-cutting standards (ESRS 1 General Requirements and ESRS 2 General Disclosures) and 10 topical standards
Materiality approach	Financial materiality	Double materiality – meaning materiality is considered on both a 'financial' and an 'impact' basis
Materiality assessment	Disclosure dependant on materiality assessment	Some mandatory disclosure requirements always to be applied and some dependant on materiality assessment
Location of reports	No prescribed approach	Prescribed structure within entities' corporate reports.
Sector-specific disclosures	Included in ISSB Standards	To be developed from 2024

Management commentary

Definition

Management commentary provides users with context through which to interpret the financial position, financial performance and cash flows of an entity.

Management commentary is not mandatory. However, the Board has produced a Practice Statement that provides guidance when producing management commentary.

Elements of management commentary

Management commentary should include information about:

- the nature of the business
- management's objectives and its strategies for meeting them
- the entity's resources, risks and relationships
- the results of operations and prospects, and
- key performance measures used by management to evaluate the entity's performance.

Exam Focus

Exam Kit questions in this area:

- Wing
- Juan
- Eloa
- Benito
- Maple
- Apaniiwa

chapter

23

Changes and developments in financial reporting

In this chapter

- Key financial reporting issues.
- Contemporary business environment.

Exam Focus

Changes and developments in financial reporting standards are an important part of to the SBR syllabus.

Key financial reporting issues

The SBR syllabus and examinable documents identify the following issues:

- digital assets
- accounting for the effects of a natural disaster
- climate change and global events
- developments related to sustainability reporting and sustainability standards (see chapter 22).

Contemporary business environment

This section covers three contemporary issues: cryptocurrency, initial coin offerings, and natural disasters.

Cryptocurrency

Definition

Cryptocurrencies are virtual currencies that provide the holder with various rights. They are not issued by a central authority and so exist outside of governmental control.

The accounting treatment of cryptocurrency is unclear. Cryptocurrency is not:

- **cash** – not readily exchangeable for goods or services
- **a cash equivalent** – risk of value change too significant
- **another type of financial instrument** – no contractual right to receive cash.

Cryptocurrency potentially falls within the scope of IAS 38 *Intangible Assets*. However this standard requires income or expense arising from fair value remeasurement to be presented in other comprehensive income rather than in profit or loss.

It may be that entities need to apply the *Conceptual Framework* (see Chapter 1) to develop an appropriate policy.

Initial coin offerings

Definition

Initial coin offerings (ICO) are a method of raising finance through cryptographic assets. Investors buy into the ICO and receive tokens in exchange.

When an entity raises funds in this way, it will record the receipt of an asset as the debit entry.

Possibilities for the credit entry include:

- **A financial liability** if the reporting entity is contractually obliged to deliver cash or another financial asset to the token recipient.
- **Equity** if the token recipient may be entitled to payments made out of distributable reserves but the reporting entity has no contractual obligation to deliver cash or another financial asset.
- **Revenue** if the recipient was a customer and a 'contract' (per IFRS 15 Revenue from Contracts with Customers) exists.
- **A provision** if there is a legal or constructive obligation to the token recipient.

Natural disasters

Some types of natural disaster, such as a floods, are becoming increasingly common. Natural disasters can have various financial reporting consequences.

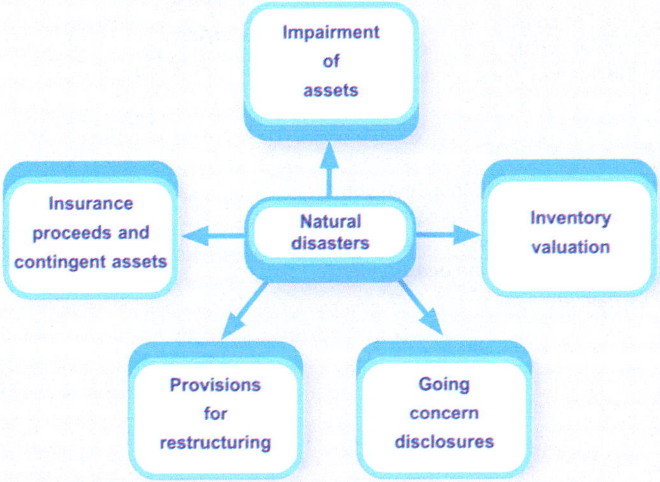

Accounting for climate change, global events and going concern assessments

Similar to natural disasters, there is no single IFRS standard that covers the impact of climate change and global events.

Companies need to consider climate-related matters and global events when the effect is material on the financial statements.

Exam Focus

In an exam question, it is important that you consider more than one IFRS standard. The scenario is likely to consider a range of issues and therefore more than one standard is likely to be relevant.

Exam Focus

Exam Kit questions in this area:

- Juan
- Wing
- Abasi
- Kimimila

References

This document references IFRS Accounting Standards, which are authored by the International Accounting Standards Board (the Board), and published in the 2024 IFRS Accounting Standards Red Book.

The Board (2024) *Conceptual Framework for Financial Reporting*. London: IFRS Foundation.

The Board (2024) IAS 1 *Presentation of Financial Statements*. London: IFRS Foundation.

The Board (2024) IAS 2 *Inventories*. London: IFRS Foundation.

The Board (2024) IAS 7 *Statement of Cash Flows*. London: IFRS Foundation.

The Board (2024) IAS 8 *Basis of Preparation of Financial Statements*. London: IFRS Foundation.

The Board (2024) IAS 10 *Events after the Reporting Period*. London: IFRS Foundation.

The Board (2024) IAS 12 *Income Taxes*. London: IFRS Foundation.

The Board (2024) IAS 16 *Property, Plant and Equipment*. London: IFRS Foundation.

The Board (2024) IAS 19 *Employee Benefits*. London: IFRS Foundation.

The Board (2024) IAS 20 *Accounting for Government Grants and Disclosure of Government Assistance*. London: IFRS Foundation.

The Board (2024) IAS 21 *The Effects of Changes in Foreign Exchange Rates*. London: IFRS Foundation.

The Board (2024) IAS 23 *Borrowing Costs*. London: IFRS Foundation.

The Board (2024) IAS 24 *Related Party Disclosures*. London: IFRS Foundation.

The Board (2024) IAS 27 *Separate Financial Statements*. London: IFRS Foundation.

The Board (2024) IAS 28 *Investments in Associates and Joint Ventures.* London: IFRS Foundation.

The Board (2024) IAS 32 *Financial Instruments: Presentation.* London: IFRS Foundation.

The Board (2024) IAS 33 *Earnings per Share.* London: IFRS Foundation.

The Board (2024) IAS 34 *Interim Financial Reporting.* London: IFRS Foundation.

The Board (2024) IAS 36 *Impairment of Assets.* London: IFRS Foundation.

The Board (2024) IAS 37 *Provisions, Contingent Liabilities and Contingent Assets.* London: IFRS Foundation.

The Board (2024) IAS 38 *Intangible Assets.* London: IFRS Foundation.

The Board (2024) IAS 40 *Investment Property.* London: IFRS Foundation.

The Board (2024) IAS 41 *Agriculture.* London: IFRS Foundation.

The Board (2024) IFRS 1 *First-time Adoption of International Financial Reporting Standards.* London: IFRS Foundation.

The Board (2024) IFRS 2 *Share-based Payment.* London: IFRS Foundation.

The Board (2024) IFRS 3 *Business Combinations.* London: IFRS Foundation.

The Board (2024) IFRS 5 *Non-current Assets Held for Sale and Discontinued Operations.* London: IFRS Foundation.

The Board (2024) IFRS 7 *Financial Instruments: Disclosure.* London: IFRS Foundation.

The Board (2024) IFRS 8 *Operating Segments.* London: IFRS Foundation.

The Board (2024) IFRS 9 *Financial Instruments.* London: IFRS Foundation.

The Board (2024) IFRS 10 *Consolidated Financial Statements.* London: IFRS Foundation.

The Board (2024) IFRS 11 *Joint Arrangements.* London: IFRS Foundation.

The Board (2024) IFRS 12 *Disclosure of Interests in Other Entities.* London: IFRS Foundation.

The Board (2024) IFRS 13 *Fair Value Measurement.* London: IFRS Foundation.

The Board (2024) IFRS 15 *Revenue from Contracts with Customers.* London: IFRS Foundation.

The Board (2024) IFRS 16 *Leases.* London: IFRS Foundation.

The Board (2024) IFRS 18 *Presentation and Disclosure in Financial Statements.* London: IFRS Foundation.

The Board (2024) IFRS 19 *Subsidiaries without Public Accountability: Disclosures.* London: IFRS Foundation.

The Board (2015) IFRS for *SMEs Standard.* London: IFRS Foundation.

The Board (2024) IFRS Practice Statement: *Management Commentary.* London: IFRS Foundation.

The Board (2024) IFRS Practice Statement: *Making Materiality Judgements.* London: IFRS Foundation.

Index

A

B

C

D

E

F

J

L

M

S

T

U

V